HERITAGE

Explore, Discover and Enjoy Beautiful Britain

Rodney
Stoke
Wookey
Hole
B3151
A371
A39
Shepton
Mallet
3
Wells
B3139
A371
A37
A361
A39
B3151
Leighton
A39
A361
Pilton
Glastonbury
2
A37
A371
Clarks
Village
A39
Street

©West One (Trade) Publishing Ltd. 1999

ISBN 1 900327 42 2 paperback

A CIP catalogue record for this book is available from the British Library.

Cartography: David Fryer
Designers: Peter Laws, Beatriz Waller
Contributor: Zoe Ross

Printed and bound in Italy.

Published by
West One (Trade) Publishing Ltd.
Portland House
4 Great Portland Street
London
W1N 5AA

Telephone: 0171 580 6886
Fax: 0171 580 9788
Email: sales@west-one.com

Contents

Foreword

For a small island country, Great Britain is extraordinarily diverse in its landscape and attractions. In the south and east are the coastal cities, towns and villages, with their romantic histories of epic voyages, smugglers and the fishing industry, where quaint fisherman's cottages are still preserved. Inland, amid some of the world's finest national parks, are landscapes dotted with stately homes, royal palaces, Roman relics, Gothic churches, meandering rivers and innumerable country walks. Britain's cities are also notable for their very individual characteristics: the medieval university colleges of Oxford and Cambridge; the wharves and waterways of Manchester; the elegant Regency architecture of Bath; and the grandeur of Edinburgh, to name but a few.

Guy Crawford
Managing Director
Heritage Hotels

Not only does Britain benefit from a long and successful history, but few other nations preserve their ancestry with such care and pride. From the mysterious ancient symbolism of Stonehenge and Avenbury, to the medieval cathedrals of Canterbury and Winchester, literature personified in Stratford and even the Industrial Revolution in the warehouses and factories of the Midlands, a tour of the country takes the visitor on a tour of the millennium, and beyond. For those with an eye more on entertainment than history, there are theme parks, zoos, racecourses and golf courses that rival any around the world.

More than 40 Heritage Hotels are dotted around the country and, with their intimate atmospheres, comfortable facilities and their own potted history within their towns or regions, can only enhance a British holiday, whether touring the country or simply taking a break in a beloved pocket of this enchanted isle.

DUAL CLIMATE CONTROL,

CRUISE CONTROL,

SUPERLOCKING DOORS

AND A LITTLE BUTTON THAT MAKES IT GO UP AND DOWN.

If Range Rovers didn't have air suspension they wouldn't be the best 4x4s in the world.

But of course they do and they are.

A Sporting Offer

For more information and to make a booking please call the hotel direct

For those of you who like their Leisure Breaks livened up with a little extra recreational activity, Heritage Hotels have got the very thing: *A Sporting Offer*. Whether your taste is for a round of golf, riding (or having a flutter whilst somebody else sits on the horse), motor racing, shooting or archery, rock climbing, a range of water sports or even ballooning, we have a hotel or inn in most parts of the country that can organise a special break for you.

Page	Location	Hotel	G	WS	F	S/A	O	H
24	Ascot	The Berystede	•			•	•	•
26	Banbury	Whately Hall			•	•	•	
28	Bath	The Bath Spa Hotel	•		•	•	•	•
30	Bath	The Francis	•		•		•	•
36	Camberley	Frimley Hall	•			•	•	•
38	Canterbury	The Chaucer Hotel	•	•				
40	Cheltenham	The Queen's						•
44	Coventry	Brandon Hall	•		•	•	•	
46	Dartmouth	The Dart Marina	•	•				
52	Dovedale	Peveril of the Peak				•	•	
60	Grasmere	The Swan	•					•
66	Hereford	The Green Dragon	•			•	•	•
76	Marlborough	The Castle & Bell	•					•
78	Marlow	The Compleat Angler	•		•	•	•	
82	Matlock Bath	The New Bath Hotel			•	•	•	
86	North Berwick	The Marine	•			•	•	
98	Ross-on-Wye	The Royal	•			•	•	
100	St Andrews	Rusacks Hotel	•		•	•	•	
102	Salisbury	The White Hart	•		•	•	•	•
104	Sherborne	The Sherborne	•			•	•	
108	Stratford-upon-Avon	The Alveston Manor	•				•	
116	Ullswater	Leeming House	•	•		•	•	•
118	Winchester	The Wessex	•	•	•	•	•	•
120	Windermere	The Old England	•	•	•	•	•	
124	Woodstock	The Bear	•			•	•	

G	Golf
WS	Water Sports
F	Flying
S/A	Shooting/Archery
O	Outdoor
H	Horseracing

Opposite page: The Dart Marina, Dartmouth.

9

List of Events

Epsom Derby

Ascot

June 1999		
5	Epsom Derby horse race	Epsom
12	Trooping the Colour	London
15/18	Royal Ascot four-day horse races	Ascot
21	Wimbledon Lawn Tennis Championship (two weeks)	Wimbledon
21	Midsummer Ritual	Stonehenge
25/27	Glastonbury Festival (three days)	Glastonbury
30	Henley Royal Regata (five days)	Henley

July 1999		
	Highland Games, throughout the month, various locations	Scotland
6/11	Hampton Court Flower Show	Hampton Court Palace
9/11	British Grand Prix	Silverstone
15/18	British Golf Open	Tayside
16	Promenade concerts (for one month)	London
20/31	Royal Tournament	London
31	National Eisteddfod (one week)	Anglesey
31	Cowes Week (one week)	Isle of Wight

August 199		
5/7	English National Sheepdog Championships	Devon
6/28	Edinburgh Military Tatoo	Edinburgh
8/30	Edinburgh Fringe festival	Edinburgh
15	Edinburgh International Festival (three weeks)	Edinburgh
26/31	Beatles International Festival	Liverpool
26/30	Glorious Goodwood horse racing	Goodwood
29/30	Notting Hill Carnival	London
29	Lord Mayor's Procession	London
30	Reading Rock Festival	Reading

September 1999		
4	Royal Highland Gathering	Braemar, Scotland
	Blackpool illuminations lit up until November	Blackpool

St Andrews, Rusacks   *Stonehenge*   *Marlow, The Compleat Angler*

10

List of Events

November 1999			
	Rugby World Cup (until January 2000)		Cardiff
5	Guy Fawkes Night fireworks	particularly spectacular in Lewes	
7	London to Brighton Veteran Car Rally		
30	St Andrew's Day celebrations		Scotland
December 1999			
31	Numerous New Year's Eve Millennium celebrations, including Hogmanay in Edinburgh and the Bath Ball in Bath		
January 2000			
1	Millennium Dome opening parade through Westminster		London
February 2000			
	Chinese New Year celebrations in London and Manchester (date varies)		
March 2000			
1	St David's Day celebrations		Wales
11/14	Crufts Dog Show		London
18	Cheltenham Gold Cup		Cheltenham
28	Oxford and Cambridge Boat Race		London
April 2000			
4	Grand National Steeplechase		Aintree
May 2000			
	Mayfest		Glasgow
	Brighton International Festival		Brighton
7/10	Badminton Horse Trials		Badminton
16	FA Cup Final		London
18/31	Hay-on-Wye Festival		Hay-on-Wye
25/29	Chelsea Flower Show		London
June 2000			
22	Millennium Mystery Plays	one month	York Minster

Gourmet dinner at the Dart Marina, Dartmouth

Edinburgh

Dartmouth, The Dart Marina

Windemere, Old England   *Silverstone.*   *Grasmere, The Swan*

Music at Leisure

For more information and to make a booking please call the hotel direct

"Music at Leisure"
weekends from £235 per person

What's included:
- free programmes
- champagne reception – Friday and Saturday evenings
- 2 nights' accommodation sharing a twin/double room with private bathroom (or single room)
- full traditional breakfast every morning
- 3 course evening meal with coffee

*A*n unrivalled opportunity for music-lovers to enjoy some of the world's best music, performed in exquisite surroundings by some of the country's most respected musicians. This year's exciting programme of recitals takes place in hotels as varied as the inspiring musical schedule itself, with each venue being renowned for its historic charm and relaxed ambience.

Why not join us for a house-party weekend of recitals by some of the world's finest musicians. The Director of Music at Leisure is Leonard Pearcey, who writes:

"We celebrate our 35th Anniversary Season in some very special settings: on the shores of Lake Ullswater and the banks of the River Thames at Marlow and the Avon at Stratford; by the magnificent cathedrals at Lincoln, Canterbury, Salisbury and Winchester; in oak-beamed inns dating back to the 13th century at Woodstock and the 15th at Lavenham; looking out at the glories of the Georgian city of Bath and the crags of the Peak District at Matlock Bath – each hotel specially chosen for its convivial ambience and relaxed charm.

Medici String Quartet

The music is as varied in time and mood as those settings: in string quartets we ride with Haydn and hunt with Mozart, mark the 25th anniversary of the death of Shostakovich and pick chrysanthemums with Puccini, serenade Spain with Borodin and Italy with Wolf, visit Britten, Tippett, Bridge and Bliss.

The piano languishes under Beethoven's *Moonlight* and Debussey's *Clair de Lune,* waltzes with Chopin and fantasises with Schumann, views Moscow with Mussorgsky and Venice and Naples with Liszt.

Music at Leisure

Then there's the flute, viola and harp of Philippa Davies and Friends, piano quintets from the Schubert Ensemble (including Schubert's *Trout* and Fitkin's *Millennium*), the wind quintet and piano of the Nash Ensemble and the strings of The Raphael (featuring sextets by Boccherini, Strauss, Tchaikovsky and Brahms).

Philippa Davies

On the Friday afternoon you settle into your room and browse through the programme notes for that evening. Then at 6.30 it's the black tie champagne reception and a meeting with fellow guests. At 7pm, the first half of the recital, with the musicians informally introducing the pieces they play; and after a champagne interval and part two they join guests for dinner.

After breakfast on the Saturday morning, a special event, then the rest of the day at leisure to explore the surrounding town or countryside, with the evening following the same pattern as the Friday, but of course with different music. Why not decide to extend your stay – or indeed arrive a day early?

With 20 more composers programmed for this 35th Anniversary Season, all in all this is a wonderful way to enjoy music, at your leisure."

Calendar of Events						
Date	**Hotel Name**	**Hotel Location**	**Musicians**	**Price**	**Telephone**	**Page ref**
Sep 10/12	The White Hart	Lincoln	Nash Ensemble	£255	0870 400 8117	74
Sep 24/26	The New Bath Hotel	Matlock Bath	Medici String Quartet	£265	0870 400 8119	82
Oct 8/10	The White Hart	Salisbury	Peter Donohow, piano	£235	0870 400 8125	102
Oct 22/24	The Wessex	Winchester	Kreutzer String Quartet	£239	0870 400 8126	118
Nov 5/7	The Chaucer Hotel	Canterbury	Alberni String Quartet	£295	0870 400 8106	38
Nov 19/21	The Bear	Woodstock	John Lill, piano	£290	0870 400 8202	124
Jan 14/16	The Bath Spa Hotel	Bath	Schubert Ensemble	£329	0870 400 8222	28
Jan 28/30	Leeming House	Ullswater	Noriko Ogawa, piano	£310	0870 400 8131	116
Feb 25/27	The Swan	Lavenham	Schidlof String Quartet	£289	0870 400 8116	72
Mar 10/12	The Compleat Angler	Marlow	Raphael Ensemble	£310	0870 400 8100	78
Mar 24/26	The Wessex	Winchester	Philippa Davies & Friends	£239	0870 400 8126	118
Apr 7/9	The Alveston Manor	Stratford	Dante String Quartet	£289	0870 400 8181	108

Break for Murder

Booking: 0345 543555 Information: 0151 924 1124 Fax: 0151 931 5505

"Break for Murder"
weekends from £190 per
person

What's included:
- welcome reception
- 2 nights' accommodation
  including dinner and full
  traditional breakfast –
  sharing a twin or double
  room, with colour TV
- tea and coffee-making
  facilities, phone, private en
  suite bathroom
- Saturday lunch
- full "Break for Murder"
  programme with
  competitions, games and
  actors

An exciting and different break, complete with stimulating entertainment, including actors, "murders plots", games and competitions. "Break for Murder" weekends run in Heritage Hotels until the end of December. Guests are advised that these weekends are not suitable for children under 16.

Imagine yourself enjoying dinner, when a stranger dramatically dies at your table. Your instincts as a mystery buff tell you that this is an obvious case of foul play. Who was he? What secrets will he take to his grave? And most importantly – who killed him?

Joy Swift is the original creator and mastermind behind Murder Weekends' now in their 19th highly successful year. Once quoted in an international magazine as "the most innovative concept in the hotel industry in the last 25 years", Joy's Murder Weekends guarantee realism, excitement and fun, but whether guests are determined to crack the case or simply want to have a good time, they are certainly never disappointed. Joy's orginal Murder Weekends are an adventure not to be missed.

Each weekend has a theme, which in the past have been as varied as weddings, award ceremonies, conferences, and will readings. There is a brand new theme and plot every four months, so if you are looking for your 2nd or 22nd Murder Weekend, you will never be disappointed by the variety and originality of the story lines.

You can assume a character before you arrive, as letters explaining the theme will be sent to you a couple of weeks before the weekend. Once the first murder has been committed, you take on another role – that of super sleuth – but will you solve the crime? The clues are abundant, the bodies are scattered, the plot so complex that you will be kept busy detecting until the early hours of Sunday.

You will arrive on Friday evening and check into your bedroom with TV and private bathroom, to relax before the weekend officially starts with a cocktail reception at 8pm, followed by a sumptuous dinner.

After the first murder, which could happen at any time on Friday night, the police will arrive and begin their investigations. You will have the advantage over them as you have already met and got to know the suspects.

After breakfast on Saturday morning, the police set up an incident room, where ever-accumulating evidence will be exhibited over the course of the

Break for Murder

weekend. You will be free in the morning to discover the attractions that the location has to offer, or you may prefer to stay in the hotel and pursue your enquiries (the actors stay in character all weekend, so even if you bump into them at the shops you can still ask them probing personal questions!). After a buffet lunch there will be some fun themed games and many more opportunities to interrogate the suspects and witness devilish doings and dastardly deaths!

On Saturday night there will be a themed party with dinner, dancing, more fun, games and of course more devious deeds and the chance to scrutinise all the clues that have amassed during the day.

On Sunday morning at 11.30, everyone is gathered together by the inspector, who presents his denouement, explaining the suspect's machination and motives. Will you have missed the vital clues that nailed the murderer or will you be one of the few super sleuths who will walk away with our coveted trophy?

The weekend officially ends at 12 noon on Sunday, but most guests stay longer, not wanting to leave and break the spell, nor say goodbye to the friends that they've made over the weekend! It is a weekend you will always remember — so take a stab at it!

To make a reservation call the hotel direct or central reservations on 0345 543555

"I can't tell you how much I enjoy the cerebral challenge your weekends pose and can only say I hope you never, ever run out of ideas."
Mrs Barnes, Boxworth, Cambs

"Well, everything went swimmingly — great hotel, great food and great to see the old gang again — that is, until the very last moment. Then Margaret solved the crime! Not only that, she was awarded a damn certificate to prove it!!! Now, she does nothing but sit watching all the detective programmes on the TV. And — you might guess — every time she solves another mystery, I get the certificate waved in my face!"
Mr & Mrs V. Garvey, Tunbridge Wells, Kent

"The weekend was packed with action, without a dull moment. The quality of the acting and the plot made it an amazing weekend. The fancy dress and games were thoroughly enjoyable. We loved every minute...Thank you, I'll definitely be back and recommend you to everyone."
Mrs Blake, Redditch, Worcs

"The six of us in our party thought that not only was the whole plot and weekend very well planned, but the execution was brilliant. The way in which your colleagues and yourself kept the whole thing going, in character and with such enthusiasm, was really first class."
Mr M. Taylor Bideford, North Devon

Calendar of Crimes					
Date	**Hotel Name**	**Hotel Location**	**Price**	**Telephone**	**Page ref**
"THE ANGEL AWARD"					
Jul 9/11	The Burford Bridge	Box Hill	£195	0870 400 8283	34
Jul 23/25	Frimley Hall	Camberley	£190	0870 400 8224	36
Aug 20/22	Whately Hall	Banbury	£190	0870 400 8104	28
Aug 27/29	The Berystede	Ascot	£195	0870 400 8111	24
"M.M.O.O.D" (Meeting the Millennium with Outstanding Optimism and Dynamism)					
Sep 24/26	Brandon Hall	Coventry	£190	0870 400 8105	44
Oct 1/3	Frimley Hall	Camberley	£190	0870 400 8224	36
Oct 8/10	The Bush Hotel	Farnham	£190	0870 400 8225	58
Oct 15/17	Alveston Manor	Stratford-upon-Avon	£195	0870 400 8181	108
Oct 22/24	The Old England	Windermere	£190	0870 400 8130	120
Oct 29/31	The Berystede	Ascot	£195	0870 400 8111	24
Nov 5/7	The Wessex	Winchester	£190	0870 400 8126	118
Nov 5/7	Brandon Hall	Nr Coventry	£190	0870 400 8105	44
Nov 12/14	The New Bath	Matlock Bath	£190	0870 400 8119	82
Nov 12/14	The Chaucer	Canterbury	£190	0870 400 8106	38
Nov 19/21	Whately Hall	Banbury	£190	0870 400 8104	26
Nov 26/28	The Berystede	Ascot	£195	0870 400 8111	24

Antique, the cognac of the House of Hine
recognised for its quality the world over.

UK Agent: Paragon Vintners Ltd, Regent Gate , Dartmouth Street, London SW1H 9BP
Tel: 0171-887 1800 Fax: 0171-887 1801

Mix *it*

Match *it*

Love *it*

Royal Doulton
has it.

Be creative with JAPORA, a practical range of fine china in a versatile design that allows you to mix and match to your heart's content. No two settings need ever be the same again.

Microwave safe

Dishwasher safe

Freezer safe

Oven safe

Chip resistant

Royal Doulton

Heritage Hotels – Abingdon
The Upper Reaches

Thames Street, Abingdon, Oxfordshire OX14 3JA See map page 4 Tel: (0)870 400 8101 Fax: (0)123 555 5182
Regional General Manager: Tony Marrinan E-mail: HeritageHotels_Abingdon.Upper_Reaches@forte-hotels.com

Honeymoon heaven for those couples who are searching for the ultimate in romance: they may just find it within the ancient walls of this small 31-bedroom hotel, which is built from a converted corn mill on an island in the Thames. Arrive by boat to dock in private moorings. All rooms overlook the Thames, and the Millwheel Restaurant (so called because of the existing millwheel in the dining room) has a traditional menu.

How to get there
Upon reaching the town centre, turn from Stratton Way into Stert Street (the A415). Those arriving by boat should be able to make their own navigational arrangements.

Facilities: 31 bedrooms with river views, 1 four-poster, 9 half-testers, hairdryer, trouser press, restaurant, bar, 2 lounges, river mooring, fresh water fishing, free car park.
Family: baby listening, baby-sitting.

Attractions: Four-poster and half-tester suites. Working millwheel in the restaurant. Nearby Wittenham Clumps inspired Winnie the Pooh. Fresh water fishing can be arranged. Blenheim Palace nearby.

Riverview Break rates
Validity dates: all dates until March 2000
Weekends May–September
£240 per person for two nights
October–April,
£220 per person for two nights
(Excludes 23–26 December and 30 December–2 January 2000)
Based on two people sharing.

Riverview Break
Arrive on Friday evening at the Upper Reaches and check into your room overlooking the River Thames. There will be flowers and champagne to greet you. Then head down to the Millwheel Restaurant for a three-course meal. Following breakfast the next morning you can travel to Oxford, which is only a 15-minute drive. There a tour of the Oxford Story attraction has been arranged, and you will be transported through the story of the university over the centuries. While in Oxford you may wish to visit the colleges, and afternoon tea has been organised at the famous Randolph Hotel for you before you return to Abingdon. No doubt, after such a busy day you will want to relax and the Millwheel Restaurant is again the setting for your evening meal. Perhaps after breakfast on Sunday you would like to stroll along the riverbank or just sit and watch the boats go by before departing.

What's included in your break:
- 2 nights' dinner, bed and breakfast in a feature river view room or suite
- champagne and flowers in your room on arrival
- 3-course dinner in the restaurant each night (wine not included in price)
- full English breakfast both days (on the terrace in summer, weather permitting).
- entry to the Oxford Story attraction (Oxford 15 minutes' drive)
- afternoon tea at the Randolph Hotel, Oxford

Abingdon

DRIVING ROUTE

Dorchester lies just off the A415 from Abingdon. Take the A415 back to Clifton Hampden, then turn right, driving south to Little Wittenham to reach Wittenham Clumps. Continue south towards Wallingford, then take the A329 to reach Beale Park. Return north on A329 and join the A417 at Streatley, continuing north to Blewbury, where the B4016 will lead to Didcot.

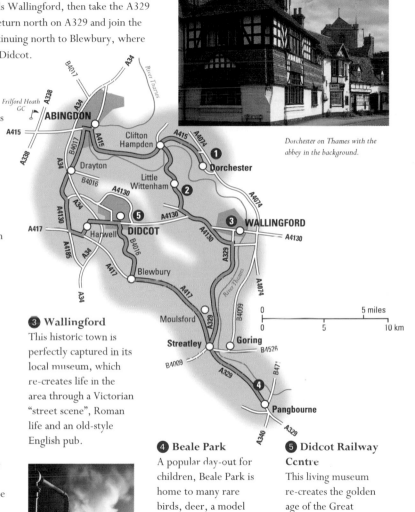

Dorchester on Thames with the abbey in the background.

❶ Dorchester on Thames

This old Roman town is dominated by its 12th-century abbey, which includes the famous Jesse Window, added to the church in the 14th century. The town's many antiques shops are its other main charm.

❷ Wittenham Clumps

The game of Poohsticks, when people throw sticks over a bridge into the flow of the water and compete to see which stick emerges first on the other side of the bridge, was immortalised in A.A. Milne's *Winnie the Pooh* stories. Wittenham Clumps is thought to be the original site mentioned by the author.

The golden age of steam is re-created at Didcot Railway Centre.

❸ Wallingford

This historic town is perfectly captured in its local museum, which re-creates life in the area through a Victorian "street scene", Roman life and an old-style English pub.

❹ Beale Park

A popular day-out for children, Beale Park is home to many rare birds, deer, a model farm and a playground. You can take trips along the River Thames here, and fish in its waters.

❺ Didcot Railway Centre

This living museum re-creates the golden age of the Great Western Railway, with steam locomotives, a broad gauge railway, and a small display of relics. Steam train rides run at weekends during the summer.

19

Heritage Hotels ~ Alfriston
The Star Inn

Alfriston, Nr Polegate, East Sussex BN26 5TH See map page 5 Tel: (0)870 400 8102 Fax: (0)132 387 0922
Regional General Manager: James Leeming E-mail: HeritageHotels_Alfriston. Star_Inn@forte-hotels.com

Prince Edward is among the guests who have visited this famous 14th-century inn, which was once a renowned meeting place for smugglers in times gone by. Oak beams and open log fires offer mellow reminders of the past and create an intimate atmosphere in the bar. Set in the South Downs, there are many fine walks, and the famous South Downs Way starts right at the door of the inn. Take in the 16-foot square church at Lullington.

How to get there
Alfriston is situated off the A25, near Polegate, East Sussex. The Star Inn lies at its heart.

Facilities: 34 bedrooms, 3 feature rooms, hairdryer, trouser press, restaurant, bar, 2 lounges, open fires in winter, free car park.
Family: baby listening, baby-sitting (on request).

Special Break rates
Validity dates: all dates until March 2000
Star Inn all-inclusive stay 3 nights and for only an extra £10 per person per night (on top of the leisure break rate) we will include morning coffee, lunch, afternoon tea, draught beer, house wine and soft drinks
(Exclude 23–26 December and 30 December–2 January 2000)

Special Break
The Star Inn is the perfect gateway to the South Downs, set in the traditional Sussex village of Alfriston. The village is just a stroll away from the Clergy House, the first National Trust property; together with the Long Man and the White Horse chalk carvings you can get a taste for the history of the region. Beachy Head, the Seven Sisters, the Cuckmere Valley and the Meanders at Exceat are some of the natural features – all within walking distance – that make this area so special. For the fit, the South Downs Way passes the doorstep for walking, mountain biking, paragliding and breathtaking views.

Attractions: Local leisure facilities — pool, sauna, tennis, squash, horse-riding and golf course. South Downs. Glyndebourne Opera House. The English Wine Centre. Drusilla's Park (for children). Herstmonceaux Science Centre. Seven Sister Cliffs. Bluebell Railway. Pevensay Castle. Beachy Head (530-foot-high cliffs).

Alfriston

After leaving the English Wine Centre in the small village of Alfriston, return to the A27 towards Lewes; Charleston Farmhouse is signposted to the left approximately two miles along this road. A further two miles along the A27 and Glyndebourne is signposted to the right. Once in Lewes, take the A275 north towards East Grinstead, and the Bluebell Railway can be found within the Sheffield Park estate. Return to the A272 towards Haywards Heath, then go south on the B2112 and A23 to Brighton.

Old cottages line the main street at Alfriston.

❶ English Wine Centre, Alfriston

Southern England has been the home of the English wine industry since Roman times. The wine centre in Alfriston includes a museum explaining the English production, with tastings of a range of award-winning wines. Staff also offer information about visiting other vineyards in the area.

❷ Charleston Farmhouse

During the early 20th century, this farmhouse was the meeting place of the group of English artists and writers known as the Bloomsbury Set. The house and gardens have been preserved as they were in their heyday.

❸ Glyndebourne

Founded in 1938, Glyndebourne is an independent opera venue and a highlight for many on the summer calendar. It is known as much for its spectacular productions, often daring in their choice of programme, as it is for the extravagant picnics enjoyed by opera buffs in its grounds.

❹ Bluebell Railway Museum

This nine-mile steam railway route north to Kingscote is a perennial favourite with both adults and children alike. The name stems from the woodlands filled with bluebells along the route.

The Indian-inspired Royal Pavilion at Brighton.

❺ Brighton

This seaside resort in many ways epitomises English holiday-making, with its ice cream sellers, deckchairs and pier. Do visit the Royal Pavilion and the charming shopping area known as "The Lanes".

21

Heritage Hotels – Amersham
The Crown

16 High Street, Amersham, Bucks HP7 0DH See map page 4 Tel: (0)870 400 8103 Fax: (0)149 443 1283
Regional General Manger: Frank Harvey E-mail: HeritageHotels_Amersham.Crown@forte-hotels.com

This glorious old coaching inn added further sheen to its glowing reputation when it made an appearance in *Four Weddings and a Funeral* with Hugh Grant and Andie MacDowell. Full timber beams, open log fires and the candlelit Courtyard Restaurant reflect the authentic Elizabethan atmosphere, and intricate hand-painted murals original to the period are miraculously preserved along with the traditional decor of the four-poster suites.

Attractions: Amersham, repeat winner of Best-Kept Village Award. Good Walking in the Chilterns countryside. Fine shopping for antiques and memorabilia. Facilities for exploring "hidden England" with trips to off-the-beaten-track

How to get there
To reach the Crown, take the A413 London Road into Old Amersham. Turn left into the High Street and you will see the hotel ahead on the left.

Facilities: 19 bedrooms, 2 four-poster mini suites, 2 twin suites, hairdryer, trouser press, restaurant, bar, lounge, open fires in winter, free car park.
Family: baby listening facilities.

Special Break rates
June–October
Ski clinic
£195 per person for two nights
Snowboarding clinic
£210 per person for two nights

November–May
Ski clinic
£185 per person for two nights
Snowboarding clinic
£200 per person for two nights
(Excludes 23–26 December and 30 December–2 January 2000)

Special Break
Visit old Amersham, a gem of England's past. Enjoy an opportunity to combine the thrill of a day's skiing or snowboarding in a forest setting with the romantic character of this 15th-century inn, as featured in the film *Four Weddings and a Funeral*.

Explore Old Amersham, which abounds in antique shops and fashionable boutiques and return to the Crown for a scrumptious afternoon cream tea in the Elizabethan lounge.

Waiting in your room will be a chilled bottle of champagne, an ideal aperitif to a three-course candlelit dinner with coffee in the Courtyard Restaurant. Round off the evening with a nightcap by a roaring fire.

Enjoy a leisurely breakfast before setting out for Summit Ski Centre near Wycombe for a fun-packed day.

Having spent an exciting day on the slopes retire to the bar for the après-ski followed by a candlelit dinner.

Refreshed, tuck into a leisurely breakfast, then prior to winding your way home visit picturesque Marlow on Thames for a riverside stroll.

What's included in your break:
• 2 nights' dinner, bed and breakfast
• a bottle of champagne on arrival in your room on the first night
• a day's clinic in skiing or snowboarding inclusive of refreshments, lunch, and equipment hire
• afternoon tea on the day of arrival

Amersham

Driving Route

Take the A404 out of Amersham and, at High
Wycombe, turn on to the A4128 to reach
Hughenden Manor. Continuing north, turn on to the
A413 towards Aylesbury. The A418 takes you to
Leighton Buzzard, where the A4012 leads on to
Woburn Abbey. Take the A5120 south towards
Dunstable. Whipsnade can be reached on the B4540,
off the A5. Return to the A5, which leads on to the
A5183 to St Albans.

❶ Hughenden Manor

The home of the 19th-century prime minister
Benjamin Disraeli is open to the public and
preserves the rooms in their Victorian
glory. The house is set in beautifully
landscaped gardens and expansive
parkland.

❷ Aylesbury

This market town is
best known for its
association with
ducks. In the 18th
and 19th centuries,
several of the town's
families, known as
"Duckers", bred a
white-feathered,
orange-footed duck that
became known as the
Aylesbury Duck.

❸ Woburn Abbey

Not in fact an abbey,
but a house, Woburn
was built in the 18th
century on the site of a
former church. Inside is
a priceless art
collection, including
works by Rembrandt.

❹ Whipsnade

One of the country's most popular zoos,
Whipsnade's inhabitants include elephants, tigers and
monkeys. The layout, which can be explored on foot
or on the zoo's own
train, allows the animals
to be kept in large
"natural" dens.

*Tigers and other residents of
Whipsnade zoo reside in large
"natural" dens.*

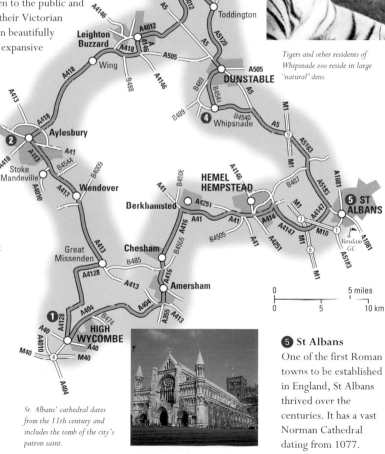

*St Albans' cathedral dates
from the 11th century and
includes the tomb of the city's
patron saint.*

❺ St Albans

One of the first Roman
towns to be established
in England, St Albans
thrived over the
centuries. It has a vast
Norman Cathedral
dating from 1077.

Heritage Hotels – Ascot
The Berystede

Bagshot Rd, Sunninghill, Ascot, Berks SL5 8HJ See map page 4 Tel: (0)870 400 8111 Fax: (0)134 487 3061
Regional General Manager: Jim Souter E-mail: HeritageHotels_Ascot.Berystede@forte-hotels.com

This old country house, set among nine acres of fine landscaped grounds, is a popular spot with golfing celebrities when playing at the Wentworth Golf Course. Try your hand at croquet on the lawn or cleave through the swimming pool before pondering the choices of the traditional English menu at Hyperion Restaurant. A favourite with sporting guests, the Diadem Bar is fashioned after a gentleman's smoking room. Later, relax in the Library Lounge (full of intriguing hidden panels) with its selection of books and, on chilly days, an open log fire.

Attractions: Murder Mystery Weekends. Royal Ascot in June. Wentworth Golf Course. Guards Polo Ground. Virginia Water Lake. Saville Gardens.

How to get there
The Berystede Hotel is on Bagshot Road, about four miles from junction 3 of the M3. Those who prefer to avoid the dubious pleasures of the motorway can reach the hotel from the A329, approximately one mile along the B3020.

Facilities: 78 bedrooms, 6 family rooms, 3 four-posters, 4 suites, 24-hour room service, hairdryer, trouser press, satellite TV, award-winning Hyperion Restaurant, oak lounge, open fires in winter, croquet lawn, outdoor heated swimming pool (May–September), putting green, free car park.
Family: baby listening.

Special Break rates
£200 per person for two nights.
£50 per room to upgrade to suite
(Excludes 23–26 December and 30 December–2 January 2000)

Special Break
A hotel since the turn of the century, the Berystede's distinctive facade – a blend of Gothic and Tudor styles – conceals a wealth of creature comforts and delights.

On arrival at the Berystede relax and enjoy afternoon tea in the Oak Lounge. Dinner will be served in the award-winning Hyperion Restaurant accompanied by a glass of wine.

Enjoy a leisurely breakfast before you take a trip to Saville Gardens, set in the grounds of Windsor Great Park. On your return there will be a seasonal plant in your room to serve as a reminder of your day.

Another chance to dine in the Hyperion Restaurant and listen to the resident pianist awaits you.

Before your departure enjoy a wholesome breakfast and perhaps pay a visit to Ascot Racecourse.

What's included in your break:
- 2 nights' dinner, bed and breakfast
- a glass of wine with dinner each evening
- afternoon tea on the day of arrival
- entrance to Saville Gardens
- seasonal potted plant

Ascot

DRIVING ROUTE

Ascot Racecourse is on the A329, one mile west of the town. Wentworth is about four miles east of Ascot, on the A30. The entrance to Windsor Great Park is on the A332. Continue along the A332 and take the A329 west to Reading. Wellington Riding is on the A33, near Riseley.

① Ascot Racecourse

For four days each June Ascot is taken over by the horse races known as Royal Ascot. The event is as much associated with fashion as it is with betting, with spectators dressed in haute couture style, most notably with large, often outrageous hats. The royal family are also in attendance, travelling down the course in open-top carriages. Other races take place in Ascot from July through to October.

② Wentworth golf course

This 18-hole golf course, dating from 1895, is one of the most renowned in England. Beautiful views, as well as professional tuition, make it popular with the general public.

Golfers practising on the putting-green of Wentworth golf club. The club is renowned, not least for the wealthy and famous who choose to play here.

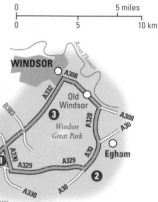

③ Windsor Great Park

This royal park, attached to the regal town of Windsor, is a beautiful location for summer picnics or an afternoon's stroll. Statues of past monarchs, such as George III, illustrate the park's heritage. Lakes, woodland and botanical flowers in the Saville Gardens add to the attractions.

Queen Elizabeth II and the Duke of Edinburgh at Royal Ascot.

⑤ Wellington Riding

One of the country's finest equestrian centres offers horse riding lessons for all levels in its indoor arena and through the surrounding woodland. Events such as dressage, hunts and gymkhanas are also held at the centre.

④ Reading

Reading was made famous by Oscar Wilde's *Ballad of Reading Gaol*, which he wrote while imprisoned in the town's penitentiary. The Reading Museum and Art Gallery is also worth a visit, not least for its copy of the Bayeux Tapestry. The annual Reading Rock Festival is one of the most popular on the calendar, and brings the town to international attention for a week each summer.

Heritage Hotels – Banbury
Whately Hall

Banbury Cross, Banbury, Oxfordshire OX16 0AN See map page 4 Tel: (0)870 400 8104 Fax: (0)129 527 1736
Regional General Manager: Tony Aspden E-mail: HeritageHotels_Banbury.Whately_Hall@forte-hotels.com

The cast of Jane Austen's *Pride and Prejudice* got into character quite easily during their stay here while filming the TV series in the area. Hidden staircases, priest holes and the resident ghost of Father Bernard are famously part of the charm of this 17th-century treasure. An oak-panelled restaurant overlooking a croquet lawn serves traditional fare in a mellow atmosphere.

How to get there
Whately Hall is very close to Banbury Cross itself. Follow the A422 for about a mile, heading west from junction 11 off the M40.

Facilities: 71 bedrooms, 5 suites, hairdryer, restaurant, bar, 2 lounges, open fires in winter, garden, croquet lawn, free car park.

Attractions: Croquet lawn. Banbury Cross. Broughton Castle (setting for TV's Pride and Prejudice*). Sulgrave Manor (where George Washington's ancestors were born). A good starting point for exploring the Cotswolds.*

Gateway to the Cotswolds rates
£135 per person for two nights
(Bonus Night: £28.50 per person)
(Excludes 23–26 December and 30 December–2 January 2000)

Gateway to the Cotswolds
Stay in the historic market town of Banbury and tour the fabulous Cotswold villages with the help of Susan Hill's book *The Spirit of the Cotswolds.*
Day 1 – Armed with your complimentary copy of the fascinating guide to the Cotswolds written by Susan Hill and an Ordnance Survey map, you can plan your tour over a leisurely breakfast. Your welcome pack will include details of many of the main attractions of the area as well as discounts for entry into some. Enjoy lunch in one of the many fine country pubs or ask for one of the hotel's picnic hampers.
Day 2 – The Cotswolds covers a large area so you may want to do some more exploring or alternatively travel a short distance north to the magnificent medieval castle of Warwick. Complimentary entry to the castle is covered and

highlights include the grounds laid out by Capability Brown through to the Royal Weekend party showing Daisy, Countess of Warwick and the "Marlborough Set" to the mighty defences of the Ramparts and Ghost Tower.

What's included in your break:
- accommodation in a twin or double room on Friday and Saturday nights
- a three-course dinner each evening
- full English breakfast each morning
- a complimentary copy of Susan Hill's book *Spirit of the Cotswolds*
- a complimentary Ordinance Survey map of the Cotswolds
- free entrance to the castle and grounds at Warwick

Banbury

DRIVING ROUTE

Broughton Castle is two miles outside of Banbury along the B4035. Drive northwest from here and take the A422 to Upton House. Sulgrave Manor is northeast of Banbury, along the B4525. Drive southeast from here and join the A43 to Silverstone. Stowe Gardens are two miles south. The A422 will lead back to Banbury.

❶ Broughton Castle

This 14th-century castle, with its attractive moat, was restored in the late 16th century and has many fine Tudor details, including panelling and furniture.

❷ Upton House

The main attraction of this house, not far from Birmingham, is the wonderful art collection and tapestries collected by the Viscount Bearsted. The terraced gardens, including a traditional kitchen garden, are also worth a stroll.

❸ Sulgrave Manor

In the 16th century Sulgrave Manor was home to a family that can count George Washington among its descendants. This connection is now the main focus of the house, and its small museum is devoted to Washington and American politics.

The circular temple at Stowe Gardens.

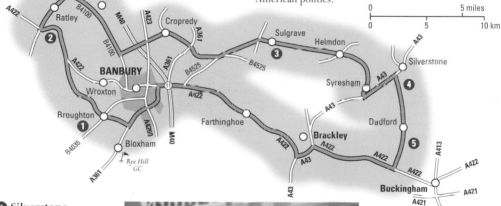

❹ Silverstone

Formula One races are held at this large racecourse, including the British Grand Prix, where the world's leading racing drivers battle it out on the track for the prestigious championship trophy.

Formula One racing cars speed round the track at Silverstone.

❺ Stowe Gardens

Landscape gardening was a passion in England in the 18th century, and Stowe is one of the finest examples – Alexander Pope was among the many who extolled its virtues.

Heritage Hotels – Bath
The Bath Spa Hotel

Sydney Road, Bath, Avon BA2 6JF See map page 3 Tel: (0)870 400 8222 Fax: (0)122 544 4006
Regional General Manager: Christopher Oakes E-mail: HeritageHotels_Bath.Bath_Spa@forte-hotels.com

Once an elegant private house, dating back to the 1830s, this hotel is fronted by a long sweeping driveway and seven acres of landscaped gardens. A light Mediterranean-style menu is served informally in the Alfresco Restaurant, amid murals and exotic plants, overlooking the gardens. The Vellore Restaurant, once a ballroom and host to the season's sparkling debutantes, now glitters with chandeliers, white napery and crystal, offering traditional English fare in an elegant setting.

How to get there
Exit the M4 at junction 18 on to the A46 following signs to Bath until the roundabout. Turn right on to the A4 following city centre signs. At the first major set of traffic lights turn left towards the A36. At the mini roundabout turn right then next left after Holburne Museum into Sydney Place. The hotel is 200 yards up the hill on the right.

Facilities: 98 bedrooms, 5 four-posters, 8 suites, 24-hour room service, mini bar, hairdryer, satellite TV, Vellore Restaurant (non-smoking), Alfresco Restaurant (non-smoking), Colonnade and Rotunda bars, drawing room, Laurels Health and Leisure Spa with indoor heated pool, gymnasium and 3 beauty rooms, hairdressing salon, croquet lawn, tennis court, chauffeur and car valet service, free car park.
Family: baby-sitting, Kemble Nursery in hotel grounds for 2–7 year olds.

Attractions: A health complex complete with solarium, sauna, massage and beauty treatments. Special Beauty and Fitness weekends. Children's nursery on-site. Croquet on the lawn. The Royal Crescent. Roman Baths. Bath Abbey.

Pure Indulgence Break
What's included in your break.
- 2 nights' accommodation
- dinner each evening in either the Alfresco or Vellore restaurants (wine not included)
- full traditional breakfast each morning
- a bottle of chilled champagne, a box of home-made chocolates and a bouquet of flowers in the room on arrival
- tickets for the open-topped bus tour of Bath

Pure Indulgence Break rates
Validity dates: all dates until 22 December 1999
Mid-week from £240 per person for two nights
Weekends from £320 per person for two nights
Upgrade to a suite or four-poster room, supplement of £150 for two nights
(rates apply to two people sharing)

Bath

From Bath, take the southeast A36 to Warminster, turning off onto the A362 via Frome to reach Longleat. Continue on the A361 to Glastonbury, then the A39 north to Wells. Cheddar can be reached on the A371, then follow the A38 north to Bristol. The A4 will lead you back to Bath. These are good, well-marked roads, but can be crowded in summer and during rush hours around the two cities.

The Clifton Suspension Bridge spans the River Avon and Gorge at Bristol.

① Longleat House and Safari Park

The country home of the Marquess of Bath, this Elizabethan mansion is open to the public. Treasures include a vast private library and a collection of Old Masters. The surrounding woodland, landscaped by "Capability" Brown, has been converted into a safari park, including lions, tigers and elephants.

② Glastonbury

The tombs of King Arthur and Queen Guinevere were thought to have been uncovered during excavation work of the town's Benedictine abbey in the 1960s, setting Glastonbury on the map forever as part of Arthurian legend. Today, the town is best known for its annual rock festival in June.

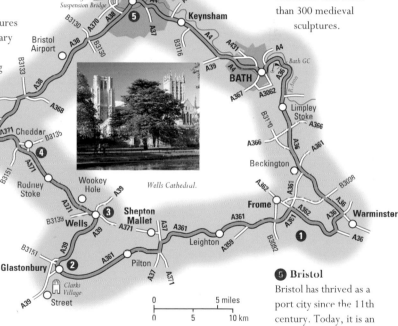

Wells Cathedral.

④ Cheddar Gorge

Huge limestone cliffs, reaching a height of 450 ft, soar above the road to the north of the town of Cheddar. The caves, forged by an underground stream, are filled with impressive stalactites and stalagmites.

③ Wells

Britain's smallest city is famed for its 13th-century cathedral, decorated with more than 300 medieval sculptures.

⑤ Bristol

Bristol has thrived as a port city since the 11th century. Today, it is an elegant city of art galleries, cafés and theatres. The Clifton Suspension Bridge, spanning the river Avon, was designed by the great engineer Isambard Kingdom Brunel.

Heritage Hotels - Bath
The Francis

Queen Square, Bath, Avon BA1 2HH See map page 3 Tel: (0)870 400 8223 Fax: (0)122 531 9715
Regional General Manager: Christopher Oakes E-mail: HeritageHotels_Bath.Francis@forte-hotels.com

The Francis is the epitome of Georgian elegance in the very heart of the city of Bath. Located in Queen Square, the hotel offers you the enviable position of being within walking distance of Bath's major attractions.

How to get there
The Francis is located in Queen Square, a short distance from the Circus. Simply follow the A4 through route, which forms the north side of Queen Square.

Facilities: 94 bedrooms, 1 suite, 2 mini suites, Edgar restaurant, Caffebar and Lounge, free car park (limited). **Family:** baby-sitting.

Attractions: Weekly antiques fair. Roman Baths. Bath Abbey. Costume Museum. The Royal Crescent. Fine Shopping.

Curtain Call Break rates
Supplement of £25 per person on the Leisure Break rates
Validity dates: Subject to availability
(Excludes 23–26 December and 30 December– 2 January 2000)

Curtain Call at the Francis on the Square Break
Combine your stay at the Francis with an evening of entertainment at the Theatre Royal, widely recognised as one of the finest provincial theatres in the country. The theatre boasts a varied programme of one-week runs, many of which are pre- or post- the West End of London. Whether you are an avid theatre-goer or an occasional enthusiast, you are sure to find plenty to choose from and for a theatre break in Bath, you cannot get closer than the Francis.
Curtain Call includes one top-price ticket for the Theatre Royal, including a glass of champagne on your return to the Francis.

Bath

WALKING ROUTE:
Bath is a compact city that is both easy and enjoyable
to explore on foot, its streets lined with ornate
architecture and fine views. No one direction is
better than another in a city of this beauty: take time
to appreciate the elegance of the streets en route to
the featured sights.

Poultney Bridge
at night.

❶ Royal Crescent
This elegant semi-circle
of houses was the
first crescent to be
built in Britain. Thirty
houses are lined with
Ionic columns along
their façades. Number 1
Royal Crescent has
been carefully restored
to reflect its original
Georgian glory.

❷ The Assembly Rooms
This fine building is
home to a fascinating
Museum of Costume,
ranging from 16th-
century clothing to
modern-day fashions.

*Any first-time trip to Bath is not
complete without a visit to the
impressive Roman Baths.*

| 0 | 110 | 220 yards |
| 0 | 100 | 200 metres |

❸ Roman Baths & Pump Room
Britain's only hot spring was turned into a
sacred site by the Romans, around which they
built these baths and a temple to serve pilgrims and
the sick. They are now the finest Roman remains in
Britain. The adjacent Pump Room was a popular
18th-century meeting place for Bath's fashionable
society, and is now a tearoom.

❹ Bath Abbey
The 16th-
century Bath
Abbey, built on the
site of a former Norman
church, is typical of the
Gothic Perpendicular
architectural style,
complete with fan
vaulting. The abbey's
tower reaches a height
of 162 ft.

❺ Poultney Bridge
No visitor to Bath can
miss the importance of
the River Avon to the
city, with its beautiful
Italianate bridge
crossing the weir.

THE ROYAL HORTICULTURAL SOCIETY

Enjoy all that's best in gardening with the RHS

Whatever the size of your garden and whatever your gardening experience, Royal Horticultural Society Membership is the perfect way to ensure that you get the very best out of your garden. As the world's premier gardening organisation, the RHS supports all that's best in gardening, bringing you year round gardening ideas and inspiration.

Outstanding benefits

As a Member of the RHS, you can enjoy unlimited free access for yourself and a guest to the magnificent RHS Gardens Wisley, Rosemoor and Hyde Hall. The famous Wisley Garden offers a fascinating blend of the beautiful with practical and innovative design and cultivation techniques. With its richly planted borders, luscious rose gardens and the exotica of the glasshouses, this garden truly captures the imagination.

RHS Garden Wisley by Derek St Romaine

A world of beautiful gardens

Join today and you can also enjoy . . .

- FREE monthly copies of *The Garden* magazine - worth £33
- FREE entry to 26 beautiful gardens nationwide
- Privileged admission to more than 20 RHS Flower Shows including the Chelsea and Hampton Court Palace Flower Shows
- FREE gardening advice from RHS experts
- And much more.

Special offer from the Royal Horticultural Society and Heritage Hotels

RHS Membership normally costs £34 for 12 months (which includes a one-off joining fee of £7). But, as a special introduction to the RHS, we would like to offer you a saving of £5 on one year's Membership - meaning you pay just £29 for a year's gardening inspiration and enjoyment.

To take advantage of this special offer, call

+44 (0)171 821 3000

quoting reference 1431. Lines are open 9am to 5.30pm (GMT), Monday to Friday. Offer ends 31 May 2000.

Millennium

COURVOISIER.

A UNIQUE BLEND, TAKING COGNAC INTO THE 21ST CENTURY
Ideal neat, over ice, mixed with tonic or ginger ale.

Heritage Hotels - Box Hill
The Burford Bridge

The Foot of Box Hill, Dorking, Surrey RH5 6BX See map page 4 Tel: (0)870 400 8283 Fax: (0)130 688 0386
Regional General Manager: James Stewart E-mail: HeritageHotels_Box_Hill.Burford_Bridge@forte-hotels.com

Every mellow brick of this ancient gem glows with history. It was here that Lord Nelson spent secret hours with his great love Emma Hamilton before going off to his last battle at Trafalgar. It nestles at the foot of a famous beauty spot, Box Hill, with Mole River running at the bottom of its spectacular gardens. Spot the clues about fellow guests in intriguing Murder Mystery Weekends.

Attractions: Tithe Barn with minstrel's gallery available for special events. Nearby Polesden Lacey (a favourite spot of the Queen Mother) whose magnificent gardens provide a summertime setting for open-air Shakespeare plays. Royal Horticultural Gardens at nearby Wisley. Ancient walks along Pilgrim's Way to Canterbury. Keats completed his great poem Endymion here. Rail to London in 40 minutes.

How to get there
Four miles from junction 9 off the M25 on the A24 at the foot of Box Hill.

Facilities: 57 bedrooms, 24-hour room service, hairdryer, trouser press, restaurant, bar, lounge, open fires in winter, heated outdoor pool (May–September), free car park.
Family: baby listening, baby-sitting.

Special Break rates
Weekends only, plus any 2 nights 21 July–30 August 1999
£160 per person for two nights (based on two people sharing)
(Excludes 23–26 December and 30 December–2 January 2000)

Special Break
Arrive at the Burford Bridge at your leisure in the afternoon. Check in to your room and enjoy a cream tea in the fabulous lounge, or, weather permitting, in the lovely gardens, and a swim in the pool.

A 3-course dinner awaits you in the one-rosette restaurant – the Emlyn Room.

Following breakfast, make your way to Denbies Wine Estate and enjoy a tour and wine tasting at this award-winning vineyard.

Then, why not take a walk up Box Hill at your leisure?

After such an enjoyable day, the Emlyn Room Restaurant is again the setting for your evening dinner. After a good night's sleep, breakfast is served before your departure. On your way home stop at Polesden Lacey to see this historic house.

What's included in your break:
- 2 nights' dinner, bed and breakfast
- champagne and flowers in your room on arrival
- 3-course dinner in the restaurant each night
- full English breakfast both days
- entry and wine tasting at Denbies Wine Estate
- entry to Polesden Lacey
- afternoon tea on arrival
- swimming pool – free entrance – 1 May–30 September, weather permitting

Box Hill

DRIVING ROUTE

Box Hill lies on the east side of the A24, Polesden Lacy sits at roughly equal distance on the west. Join the A246 at Leatherhead, and Clandon Park is at the junction with the A247. Take the A25 through Dorking, and take the B2032, B2220 and B290 to Chessington. Continue north along the B290 to Epsom.

❷ Polesden Lacy

This Regency house, built in the 1820s, was the home of the society hostess, Mrs Ronnie Greville at the turn of the 20th century. Visited by royalty and the rich and famous, Polesden Lacy was the site of high society partying.

❸ Clandon Park

This Palladian villa, inspired by the Italian architect Andrea Palladio, was built in the 18th century for the Onslow family. Inside the house is a fine collection of English porcelain. The impressive grounds around the house include a Maori meeting house, which the Earl of Onslow brought back with him from New Zealand in the 19th century.

❶ Box Hill

This tall mound in the heart of Surrey has always been a popular day-trip location, not least for its fine views across the county. In winter, both children and adults can be seen "sledging" down the slopes when the hill is covered with snow.

The Epsom Derby is one of the top events in British horse racing.

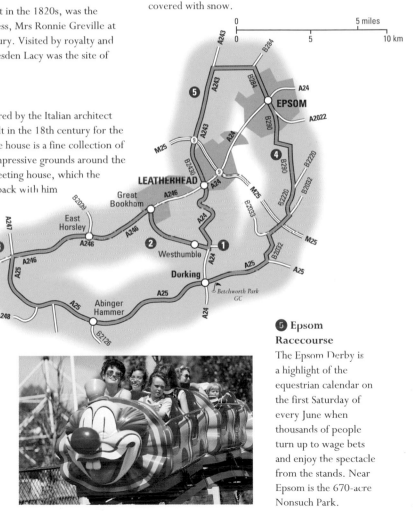

❹ Chessington World of Adventures

Once little more than a zoo, Chessington is now one of England's major theme parks and, from April to October, buzzes with excited children and thrill-seeking adults.

The Circus World roller coaster and other rides make a trip to Chessington World of Adventures a fun day out for the whole family.

❺ Epsom Racecourse

The Epsom Derby is a highlight of the equestrian calendar on the first Saturday of every June when thousands of people turn up to wage bets and enjoy the spectacle from the stands. Near Epsom is the 670-acre Nonsuch Park.

Heritage Hotels – Camberley
Frimley Hall

Lime Ave, off Portsmouth Road, Camberley, Surrey GU15 2BG See map page 4 Tel: (0)870 400 8224 Fax: (0)127 669 1253
Regional General Manager: James Stewart E-mail: HeritageHotels_Camberley.Frimley_Hall@forte-hotels.com

How to get there
Leave the M3 at junction 3 and follow the A30 west to the Mongolian Barbecue. Branch left on to the A325 and then turn right into Conifer Drive and Lime Avenue to the Frimley Hall Hotel.

Facilities: 86 bedrooms, 1 four-poster, 1 tester, 3 half-canopies, 15 family bedrooms, hairdryer, trouser press, Wellington Restaurant, bar, free car park.
Family: baby listening.

This is a classic ivy-clad Victorian manor set in four acres of beautiful gardens with green velvety lawns. Its timeless air and gracious setting are just half an hour from Heathrow Airport and are guaranteed to have a calming effect on the ragged nerves of any jet-lagged business executives. Or those getting married: you can now have both the wedding ceremony and the reception at Frimley Hall. Or simply settle for a drink in the Sandhurst Bar and a fine traditional meal in the Wellington Restaurant. A grand, ornately carved staircase leads to rooms with leaded windows and inlaid mahogany furniture.

Attractions: Close to Royal Military Academy at Sandhurst. (An old staging post is nearby where highwaymen used to lie in wait.) Jane Austen's house at Chawton (where she completed Pride and Prejudice). Loseley Park. Clandon Park. Thorpe Park. Windsor. The Royal Horticultural Gardens at Wisely. Local leisure facilities: indoor swimming pool, squash, gym, snooker, table tennis, horse-riding and golf.

Special Break rates
Weekends only, plus any 2 nights 21 July–30 August 1999
£150 per person for two nights (based on two people sharing)
(Excludes 23–26 December and 30 December–2 January 2000)

Special Break
Arrive at Frimley Hall at your leisure in the afternoon. Check in to your room and enjoy a cream tea in the fabulous lounge.

A 3-course dinner awaits you in the Wellington Restaurant.

Following breakfast, make your way to Wisley Gardens and enjoy a gentle, or not so gentle, walk around the extensive grounds owned by the Royal Horticultural Society.

After such an enjoyable day, the Wellington Restaurant is again the setting for your evening dinner. After a good night's sleep, breakfast is served before your departure. On your way home stop at Birdworld at Farnham to see the many exotic birds together with the many other attractions at this venue.

What's included in your break:
• 2 nights' dinner, bed and breakfast
• champagne and flowers in your room on arrival
• 3-course dinner in the restaurant each night
• full English breakfast both days
• entry to Wisley Gardens
• entry to Birdworld
• afternoon tea on arrival

Camberley

DRIVING ROUTE

Sandhurst lies two miles northwest of Camberley on the A321. From here, take the A30 and A319 to Chobham, then take the A3046, A245 and the B367 to Wisley, which sits on the A3. Follow the A3 south to Guildford and turn off to the left to reach Loseley Hall. Rejoin the A3 then take the A31 to Runfold and the North Downs Way is marked to your left. The A331 leads north to Aldershot and Farnborough.

Rhododendron bushes in full flower at Wisley Gardens.

❶ Sandhurst

This small town is best known for the Royal Military Academy. Its harsh regime to produce the finest and the best soldiers is part of English lore. The Academy Museum, which includes exhibits of uniforms and medals of Imperial armies, is particularly popular with children.

❷ Wisley Gardens

These beautiful gardens were created in 1878 as an experiment in growing "difficult" plants. Collections of plants from around the world still thrive in this unlikely spot, including rock gardens, alpine gardens and Japanese gardens, as well as modern-style gardens.

❸ Loseley Hall

The 16th-century home of the More family abounds with original Tudor details such as panelling, plaster ceilings and a Great Hall. Elizabeth I and James I both stayed here. Today, the house is given over to a highly successful dairy industry. Visits to the dairy farm, including watching the milking of the cows, are part of the attraction.

❹ North Downs Way

The North Downs Way is a spectacular walking route that stretches from Farnham to the coast in Kent. En route are beautiful views of the Surrey countryside, past rivers and valleys. The path is negotiable by walkers of any capability.

Military aircraft are put through their paces once a year at the Farnborough air show.

❺ Aldershot Military Museum

This museum exhibits details of military life in the area since 1854. Army transport from horses to World War II armoured carriers are also on display. Nearby Farnborough is the site of the annual airshow, a highlight for anyone with an interest in aerospace.

Heritage Hotels - Canterbury
The Chaucer Hotel

Ivy Lane, Canterbury, Kent CT1 1TU See map page 5 Tel: (0)870 400 8106 Fax: (0)122 745 0397
Regional General Manger: James Leeming E-mail: HeritageHotels_Canterbury.Chaucer_Hotel@forte-hotels.com

Originally a private Georgian house standing opposite Canterbury's ancient city walls. All the *en-suite* bedrooms in this historic hotel are named after Chaucer's characters. Canterbury is deeply woven into the fabric of English history and even before medieval times it had always attracted religious pilgrims, a tradition now revitalised by the ever-present Millennium.

How to get there
Canterbury is situated 10 miles from the end of the M2. The Chaucer is in Ivy Lane, on the left of Lower Chantry Lane, on the eastern side of the city wall.

Facilities: 42 bedrooms, hairdryer, trouser press, restaurant, bar/lounge, free car park.
Family: baby listening, baby-sitting.

Special break validity dates
Weekends only from June 1999–end March 2000 (Excludes 23–26 December and 30 December–2 January 2000)

Special Break
Stay two nights at the weekend on the leisure break rate and you'll receive two free tickets to enjoy the Canterbury Tales, one of Britain's most popular attractions.

A visit to Canterbury Tales is just like returning to medieval England, with its stunning reconstructions of 14th-century Canterbury. Inside this historic building you can step back into medieval Canterbury with all its splendours. Here you can join Geoffrey Chaucer (the hotel's namesake and England's finest poet) and his colourful characters as they journey towards the shrine of St Thomas Becket and Canterbury Cathedral.

Attractions: Canterbury Cathedral. Canterbury Tales Museum, a medieval adventure. St Augustine's Abbey (6th-century ruins). Nearby Leeds Castle and 500-acre parkland. Gateway to "The Garden of England" countryside. Goodestone Park. Punt trips on the river. Nature reserves at Graveney Marshes, Wyr and Crundale Downs. Good shopping.

Canterbury

DRIVING ROUTE

Take the A28 out of Canterbury to Ashford, and join the M20 until junction 8, exiting to reach the grounds of Leeds Castle. The A274 south joins the A262 at Biddenden, where Sissinghurst is located three miles to the east. Take the A229 and B2086 to Rolvenden, and join the A268 to Rye. The A259 joins the B2011 at Folkestone, leading to Dover. The A2 is a direct route back to Canterbury.

Leeds castle in autumn.

❶ Canterbury Cathedral

The head site of the Church of England, Canterbury Cathedral was begun in 1070 and still dominates the city. The shrine of Thomas à Becket commemorates the assassinated saint who formed the subject for T.S. Eliot's *Murder in the Cathedral*. There are abundant decorative features from the 14th to the 16th centuries.

❷ Leeds Castle

This Norman fortress is best known for its magnificent setting, half on an island in the middle of a lake and surrounded by gardens and a traditional English maze. Once a royal property, the castle is now used for social functions.

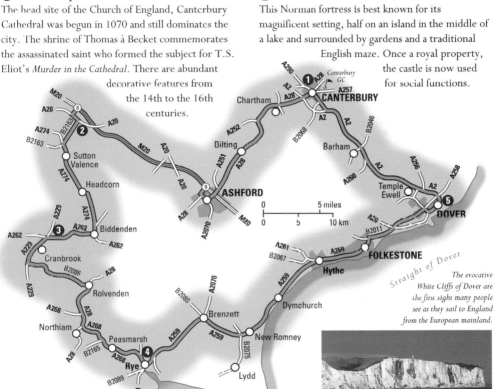

Straight of Dover

The evocative White Cliffs of Dover are the first sight many people see as they sail to England from the European mainland.

❹ Rye

One of the most picturesque towns in England achieves most of its charm from its hilly layout and cobbled streets. Tudor buildings, medieval churches and a small castle all add to the atmosphere.

❸ Sissinghurst

The grounds of this Elizabethan manor were lovingly landscaped into one of England's finest gardens. Separate areas have different "themes", such as the "White Garden", with white and silver flowers.

❺ Dover

First established as a town by the Romans, today Dover's main attraction is its 12th-century castle complex. From the top of the Keep there are views across the English Channel to France. Dover is also known for its White Cliffs, the last coastal view of England as you sail across to the European mainland.

Heritage Hotels – Cheltenham

The Queen's

The Promenade, Cheltenham, Gloucestershire GL50 1NN See map page 7 Tel: (0)870 400 8107 Fax: (0)124 222 4145
Regional General Manager: Tony Aspden E-mail: HeritageHotels_Cheltenham.Queens@forte-hotels.com

This elegant hotel commands a spectacular position at the top of the tree-lined promenade of Cheltenham Spa. The town itself is the most complete Regency Town in Britain with over 2000 listed buildings and is the gateway to the picturesque Cotswolds. The Queen's is renowned as a venue for traditional afternoon teas in the lounge, and top chef Raymond Blanc's Le Petit Blanc brasserie provides an exciting and informal alternative to the more serene setting of the hotel's Napier Restaurant.

Attractions: Browse around the chic shops of Cheltenham and admire the town's fine architecture. Take "The Romantic Road" and explore the beautiful towns and villages of the Cotswolds. Visit the racecourse – the home of the Cheltenham Gold Cup. Enjoy the Festival of Literature in October or the Music Festival in July. Take a trip to Gloucester docks and discover the history of the Inland Canals at the National Waterways Museum. Explore the many parks and gardens in the area, including Sudeley Castle.

How to get there

The Queen's is close to the town centre, just opposite the Ladies' College and at the junction of the Promenade and Imperial Square.

Facilities: 73 rooms, 2 four-poster rooms, 4 executive feature rooms, 24-hour room service, hairdryer, trouser press, satellite TV, Napier Restaurant, Le Petit Blanc Restaurant, bar, lounge, garden views, free car park (for residents). Guests on dinner-inclusive rates dine in the Napier Restaurant.
Family: baby listening, baby-sitting.

Wine & Water Break rates

£175 per person for two nights
Bonus Night (Sunday): £45 per person
(Excludes 23–26 December and 30 December–2 January 2000)

Wine & Water Break

A weekend with a difference, mixing the fascinating world of wine-making with the history of British waterways.
Day 1 – A short car journey to Newent takes you to the Three Choirs Vineyard in the glorious Gloucestershire countryside. Your visit includes a tour of the vineyard with a video presentation and tasting followed by a delicious lunch in the Vineyard Restaurant, which has been awarded two AA rosettes.
Day 2 – Visit Gloucester Docks, the most inland port in Britain. The docks have now been subject to a gentle and thoughtful restoration programme, which has included the development of the National Waterways Museum. This award-winning museum tells the 200-year story of the inland waterways through lively displays and interactive exhibits.

You will enjoy exploring the five-floored antiques centre and entry has also been arranged into the Robert Opie Collection, a nostalgic look at advertising and packaging, where you can see the packs, bottles and tins of your childhood.

What's included in your break:
- accommodation in a twin or double room on Friday and Saturday
- 3-course dinner each evening
- full English breakfast each morning
- tour, tasting and lunch at Three Choirs
- entrance to the National Waterways Museum and the Robert Opie Collection
- a mixed case of Three Choirs wines delivered direct to your home on your return

Cheltenham

DRIVING ROUTE

The A46 south out of Cheltenham leads directly to Painswick and then on to Stroud. The A419 joins the M5 at junction 13; exit onto the A38 at junction 12 to reach Gloucester. Follow the A38 and A4019 back to Cheltenham. Sudeley Castle lies outside the town of Winchcombe on the B4632, which also leads back to Cheltenham.

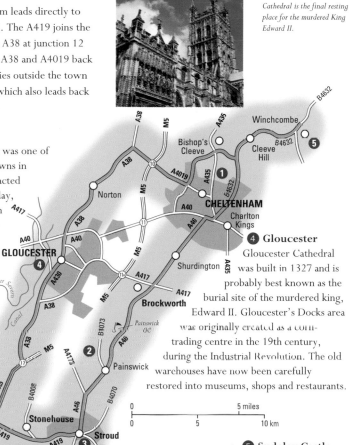

The 14th-century Gloucester Cathedral is the final resting place for the murdered King Edward II.

❶ Cheltenham

In the 19th century Cheltenham was one of the most popular and elegant towns in England, high society being attracted by its restorative spa water. Today, the town is probably best known for its racecourse, which buzzes in March during its National Hunt Festival.

❷ Painswick

This pretty, old town originally grew up around the wool industry, but today its main attraction is the restored 18th-century Rococo Garden, where the plants are laid out and pruned to unusual but attractive designs.

❸ Stroud

England's cloth, wool and textile industries were all largely centred around Stroud and many of its former mills are still standing, some now converted in to luxury loft-style accommodations. A small museum in the town details the industrial history.

The elegant Cheltenham Promenade in the summer.

❹ Gloucester

Gloucester Cathedral was built in 1327 and is probably best known as the burial site of the murdered king, Edward II. Gloucester's Docks area was originally created as a corn-trading centre in the 19th century, during the Industrial Revolution. The old warehouses have now been carefully restored into museums, shops and restaurants.

❺ Sudeley Castle

Sudeley Castle has strong connections with the British monarchy – Charles I found refuge here during the Civil War and, some years earlier, the last of Henry VIII's six wives, the widowed Catherine Parr, lived here as the wife of Lord Sudeley. Various artefacts within the house document its rich past.

Heritage Hotels - Chester

Blossoms Hotel

St John's Street, Chester, Cheshire CH1 1HL See map page 7 Tel: (0)870 400 8108 Fax: (0)124 434 6433
Regional General Manager: Debbie Johnson E-mail: HeritageHotels_Chester.Blossoms@forte-hotels.com

Blossoms lies at the very heart of the medieval walled city of Chester. Its popularity dates back to the last century, when Chester became an area for fashionable folk who demanded elegant, spacious accommodation. The same atmosphere remains here, amid high ceilings, a sweeping staircase, potted plants, and the scene-setting music from the pianist in the Brookes Restaurant.

How to get there

From junction 12 of the M53 follow signs for the city centre. St John's Street is off Eastgate Street (which is signposted from the ring road) at the centre of the shopping and pedestrianised area.

Facilities: 64 bedrooms, 1 suite, 1 four-poster, 1 half-tester, room service, hairdryer, restaurant, bar, lounge, NCP car park nearby (special free 24-hour pass provided by hotel).
Family: baby listening, baby-sitting.

Attractions: A walk along the walls is not to be missed. Shadstone Castle. Chirk Castle; Erdigg Hall. Sandy beaches of North Wales coastline.

Special Break rates

Price per person, £140 for two nights
(Excludes 23–26 December and 30 December–2 January 2000)

Special Break

Blossoms lies at the very heart of the medieval walled city of Chester. It was once the terminus of the London to Chester coach ("stand and deliver!"). Chester dates back to Roman times and the ancient sandstone Cathedral is worthy of a visit, while a walk along the walls is an experience not to be missed.

Enjoy a 3-course evening meal in either the stylish Brookes Restaurant or in the new Mongolian Barbecue Restaurant.

After a leisurely breakfast the next day, take a walk on the wild side! Visit the largest zoo in the country, home to many rare animals, open every day except Christmas day. A fun day out for everyone. Return to the hotel for your evening meal.

On the second day of your stay, after enjoying your breakfast, why not take an open-top bus tour of the city. A truly unique way to enjoy this historic city.

What's included in your break:
• 2 nights' dinner, bed and breakfast
• tickets for the open-top bus tour of the city
• tickets to the zoo for 2 adults and up to 2 children
• free accommodation for children sharing adults' room
• free meals for all children under the age of 5

Chester

DRIVING ROUTE

The A41 leads from Chester to Ellesmere Port. Then take the M56 to junction 12 and go south along the A533 and A556 to Knutsford. Return north along the A556/56 to Salford. The Granada Studios are in Castlefield, a suburb of Manchester along this road.

❶ Chester

The Tudor timbered buildings are the overriding image of this attractive northern town. Its history goes back further, to Roman times, and part of an old amphitheatre from this era can also be seen.

❷ Ellesmere Port

The prosperity of Chester stemmed from its access to canal and sea routes, making trading possible. The boat museum at Ellesmere Port details the history of canals and has a large number of historic barges on display.

❸ Knutsford

Dating back to the Vikings, Knutsford is now best known as the home of the 19th-century novelist Elizabeth Gaskell. She used the town as the basis of her novel Cranford. Close to Knutsford is the Jodrell Bank Observatory, one of the world's largest radio astronomy. The giant radio telescopes track spacecraft and satellite and study the radio universe.

Giant radio telescope at the Jodrell Bank Observatory, near Knutsford.

❹ Salford

The early 20th-century artist Lowry encapsulated the industrial landscape of Manchester in his highly individual works of "matchstick" workers. His home town is now given over to a fine art gallery, which exhibits some of his best paintings.

❺ Granada Studios

Undoubtedly Manchester's most popular visitor attraction. A tour of these television studios includes a visit to the set of Coronation Street, the long-running soap opera set in a fictional suburb of the city.

Eastgate clock in Chester.

Heritage Hotels – Coventry
Brandon Hall

Brandon, Warwickshire CV8 3FW See map page 8 Tel: (0)870 400 8105 Fax: (0)120 354 4909
Regional General Manager: Tony Aspden E-mail: HeritageHotels_Coventry.Brandon-Hall@forte-hotels.com

An impressive tree-lined avenue forms the driveway to this 17th-century hotel set in 17 acres of woodland, once a shooting lodge belonging to Brandon Manor. The historic village is mentioned in the Domesday Book, and the Lodge's own sporting traditions continue with facilities for clay pigeon shooting, archery and croquet on the lawn.

Attractions: Close to the fabulous castle of Warwick, where you can enjoy one of the many events weekends such as jousting and long-bow shooting. Warwick Castle also boasts a fine tableau of life at the castle by the world-famous Madame Tussauds. Visit the Regency Spa Town of Leamington. The hotel is convenient for the NEC and Birmingham city centre and the NIA as well as Shakespeare's Stratford.

How to get there
Brandon sits on the A428, reachable via the A46 from the North or A45 from the South. Once on either the A45 or A46 follow the signs for Binley Woods into Brandon. At the foot of the hill fork to the right past a garage, the hotel is 300 yards on the right.

Facilities: 57 bedrooms, 1 four-poster, 2 executive feature rooms, 1 mini suite, restaurant, bar, lounge, 6-court squash club, open fire in winter, mini golf and croquet (summer only), clay pigeon shooting and archery (available on request and subject to minimum group size), free car park.
Family: baby listening, baby-sitting by prior arrangement.

Britain's Motoring Heritage Break rates
£135 per person for two nights
Bonus night: £28.50 per person
(Excludes 23–26 December and 30 December–2 January 2000)

Britain's Motoring Heritage Break
Come and explore the rich history of the motor industry in the Midlands while enjoying the wonderful food and relaxing atmosphere of Brandon Hall.
Day 1 – Visit the fascinating Coventry Motor Museum with its large collection of vehicles depicting the history of the city's motoring heritage. Step back in time with the fine collection of Vintage cars including Queen Mary's Daimler and come right up to date with the amazing Thrust II. A delicious picnic hamper with complimentary Thermos flask and picnic rug is provided so that after your visit you can drive out into some of Warwickshire's beautiful countryside for your lunch.
Day 2 – After a hearty breakfast you have a choice of two visits. Motor cycling enthusiasts can

visit the National Motorcycle Museum between Coventry and Birmingham and admire some of the bikes that once led the world in engineering design. Alternatively there is the largest collection of historic British cars in the UK at The Heritage Motor Centre at Gaydon.

What's included in your break:
• accommodation in a twin or double room on Friday and Saturday night, 3-course dinner each evening and full English breakfast each morning
• entrance to Coventry Motor Museum and either the Heritage Motor Centre or the National Motorcycle Museum
• complimentary Thermos flask and picnic rug

Coventry

DRIVING ROUTE

The A428 leads from Brandon into the centre of
Coventry, dominated by its cathedral. Leave the city
northward on the A444 and turn off at Fenny
Drayton to reach Bosworth Battlefield. Follow the
B582 and A47 into Leicester. The A607 leads out of
the city eastwards to Melton Mowbray.

❶ Coventry Cathedral

During World War II, Coventry suffered more than
any other city in England, and was virtually flattened
by bombs from the Luftwaffe in 1940. In 1962 Sir
Basil Spence built a new cathedral on the old site,
which is considered one of the finest postwar
buildings in the country. Modern stained glass and
religious art add to the spectacle.

❷ Bosworth Battlefield

In 1485, Bosworth was
the historic site of the
battle between
Richard III and the
eventual victor, the
future Henry VII.
Today a visitors'
centre recounts the
life and times of
these warring
monarchs and
details of their
battle.

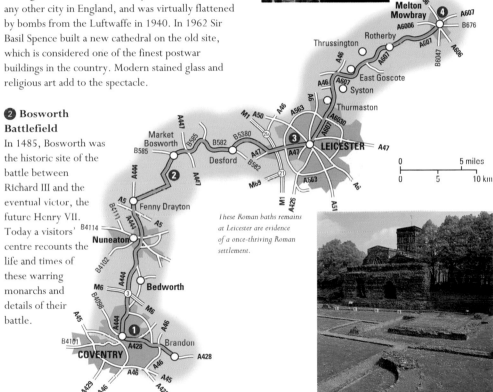

These Roman baths remains
at Leicester are evidence
of a once-thriving Roman
settlement.

❸ Leicester

A thriving Roman settlement in turn led to an
important medieval town and the homes of the
influential Earls of Leicester. Today the city is known
for its large Asian community, who enhance the city
with spicy aromas from the many curry houses and,
during their Festival of Light (Diwali) in October,
with fairy lights along the streets.

❹ Melton Mowbray

The quintessentially English snack, the pork pie
(minced pork covered in aspic and pastry) was
created by the huntsmen of Melton Mowbray.
Despite changing opinions on fox-hunting, the pies
are still made here and enjoyed by millions around
the country.

Heritage Hotels – Dartmouth
The Dart Marina

Sandquay, Dartmouth, South Devon TQ6 9PH See map page 3 Tel: (0)180 383 2580 Fax: (0)180 383 5040
Regional General Manager: Kim Yardley E-mail: HeritageHotels_Dartmouth.Dart_Marina@forte-hotels.com

This part of England is forever linked with the name of Sir Francis Drake, England's famous seafaring hero who simply didn't recognise stress. He took time to finish his game of bowls and still beat the Spanish Armada. The theme of sea and sailing continues at the Dart Marina. All the bedrooms overlook the River Dart and the exclusive marina, as do the restaurant, lounge and terrace, which have superb views. Fresh fish landed at Brixham happens to be one of the hotel's many specialities. For an undisturbed view of the sailing craft, book one of the rooms with a balcony on the second floor.

How to get there
Motorists should take the A3122 from Totnes into Dartmouth. The road becomes College Way just before the Higher ferry, and the Dart Marina is on the left in Sandquay Road.

Facilities: 50 bedrooms with stunning views, room service, hairdryer, trouser press, restaurant, riverside terrace, bar, lounge, free car park.
Family: baby listening, baby-sitting.

Attractions: Dartmoor. Buckfast Abbey. Dart Valley Railway's steam locomotives. Totnes, a Tudor town where locals dress as Elizabethans on summer Tuesdays. Bird sanctuary at Slapton Ley. Dartmouth harbour. Torbay beaches. Local leisure facilities: indoor swimming pool, sauna, tennis, squash, gym, snooker, table tennis, horse-riding and golf course.

English Heritage Break rates
Validity dates: Tuesday to Saturday, November 1999–March 2000
£150 per person for a 2-night break (based on two people sharing)
(Excludes 23–26 December and 30 December–2 January 2000)

English Heritage Break
Arrive at your leisure at the Dart Marina to a Devon cream tea and check into your room with stunning views of the River Dart. There will be a gift of local Dartington glass in your room to welcome you. A 3-course dinner will be served in Hauley's Restaurant featuring many fish specialities from Brixham quay with a fine bottle of Chablis to complement the meal.

During your 2-day break you will have the opportunity to explore the historic town of Dartmouth, dominated by the Britannia Royal Naval College, and walk the many footpaths on the magnificent coastline. There will be complimentary tickets to both Dartmouth and Totnes castles, open between 10am and 4pm Wednesday to Sunday.

What's included in your break:
- 2 nights' accommodation in a room with a river view
- a gift of Dartington glass
- 3-course dinner in Hauley's award-winning restaurant each night
- a bottle of Chablis or wine of your choice with dinner each evening
- traditional English breakfast each morning
- Devon cream tea on arrival
- tickets to Dartmouth Castle and Totnes Castle

Dartmouth

DRIVING ROUTE

A ferry across the Dart Estuary leads to the A379 and on to Brixham, then Paignton. Torquay sits about three miles further north along the same road. The best route from here into the heart of the Dartmoor National Park is the A380, joining the A382 at Newton Abbot. The B3357 joins the B3212 at Two Bridges, then the A386 leads south to Plymouth.

① Brixham

The fishing industry has made this pretty coastal town famous, and sampling the fish and chips in one of the many restaurants is a highlight of any visit. Another attraction is the reconstruction of Sir Francis Drake's ship the Golden Hind, moored at the quay.

② Paignton & Dartmouth Steam Railway

This seven-mile steam train journey chuffs along the coast then along the estuary, to Kingswear.

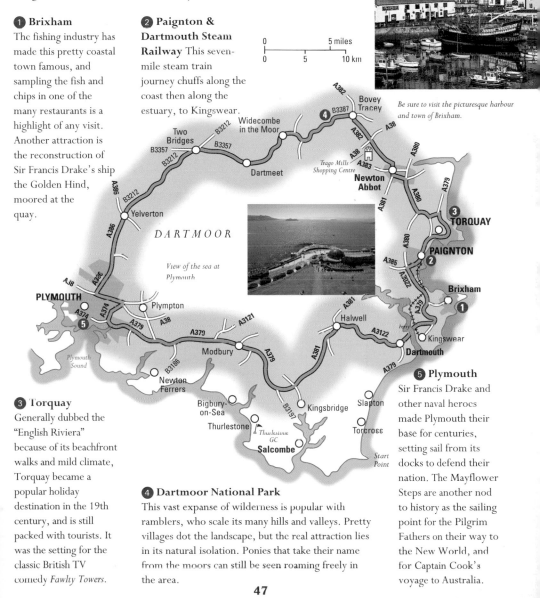

Be sure to visit the picturesque harbour and town of Brixham.

View of the sea at Plymouth

③ Torquay

Generally dubbed the "English Riviera" because of its beachfront walks and mild climate, Torquay became a popular holiday destination in the 19th century, and is still packed with tourists. It was the setting for the classic British TV comedy *Fawlty Towers*.

④ Dartmoor National Park

This vast expanse of wilderness is popular with ramblers, who scale its many hills and valleys. Pretty villages dot the landscape, but the real attraction lies in its natural isolation. Ponies that take their name from the moors can still be seen roaming freely in the area.

⑤ Plymouth

Sir Francis Drake and other naval heroes made Plymouth their base for centuries, setting sail from its docks to defend their nation. The Mayflower Steps are another nod to history as the sailing point for the Pilgrim Fathers on their way to the New World, and for Captain Cook's voyage to Australia.

47

Getting Away with Murder

ENJOY A WEEKEND OF ORGANIZED MAYHEM, SOLVING A MADLY MALICIOUS MURDER IN THE COMFORT AND CHARM OF AN HISTORIC HERITAGE HOTEL.

Super sleuths and Sherlock Holmes devotees will delight in *Heritage Hotels' Murder Weekends*, an opportunity to pit your detecting skills against the talents of our nasty creators of original murder plots. Book your place in a Heritage Hotel of choice, and you will receive details of your role and the murder theme (a wedding, a will reading, an award ceremony, and so on) well in advance. Once you arrive, the clues are abundant, the bodies scattered, and the plot so complex you will be busy detecting from Friday evening to the final denouement on Sunday noon. Amidst all this mayhem, you will be pampered with wonderful service, heaps of ambiance, delicious meals and a cocktail (or three!)

Do you have time to kill? Join us for a Heritage House Murder Weekend. We're dying to see you. To book, call central reservations on 034 554 3555 or call individual hotels directly.

THE VERY ESSENCE
OF BURGUNDY

"THE WINES OF THIS GREAT
BURGUNDY HOUSE CONSISTENTLY
PROVE THEIR UNMISTAKABLE CLASS."
TOM STEVENSON

Heritage Hotels – Dorking
The White Horse

High Street, Dorking, Surrey RH4 1BE See map page 4 Tel: (0)870 400 8282 Fax: (0)130 688 7241
Regional General Manager: James Stewart E-mail: HeritageHotels_Dorking.White_Horse@forte-hotels.com

With its old oak beams, open log fires and inviting lounge with nooks for quiet conversation, there is a positively Dickensian flavour about this beautiful old coaching inn. In fact, Charles Dickens was a visitor and did some of his writing here. The bedrooms feature two four-poster rooms, as welcoming as the restaurant with its traditional English menu.

How to get there
To reach the White Horse, leave the M25 at junction 9, and take the A24 towards Leatherhead and Dorking. After four miles, take the third exit at the roundabout to Dorking town centre. Follow the High Street for 600 yards, the hotel is on your left.

Facilities: 70 bedrooms, 2 four-posters, 2 half-testers, hairdryer, trouser press, bar, restaurant, open fires in winter, free car park.
Family: baby listening.

Attractions: Dorking town full of antique shops. Nearby Denby's Vineyards, for the UK's award-winning English wines. Chessington, a theme park and zoo. Leith Hill, the highest point on the Downs. Nearby Epsom for race events.

Special Break rates
Weekends only, plus any 2 nights 21 July–30 August 1999
£150 per person for two nights (based on two people sharing)
(Excludes 23–26 December and 30 December–2 January 2000)

Special Break
Arrive at the White Horse at your leisure in the afternoon. Check-in to your room and enjoy a cream tea in the fabulous lounge. A 3-course dinner awaits you in the restaurant.

Following breakfast, make your way to Denbies Wine Estate and enjoy a tour and wine tasting at this award-winning vineyard.

Then, why not take a walk up Box Hill at your leisure?

After such an enjoyable day, the restaurant is again the setting for your evening dinner.

Following a good night's sleep, breakfast is served before your departure. On your way home stop at Polesden Lacey to see this historic house.

What's included in your break:
- 2 nights' dinner, bed and breakfast
- champagne and flowers in your room on arrival
- 3-course dinner in the restaurant each night
- full English breakfast both days
- entry and wine tasting at Denbies Wine Estate
- entry to Polesden Lacey
- afternoon tea on arrival

Dorking

DRIVING ROUTE

Leith Hill leads off the A24 south of Dorking. Continue along the A24 and take the B2037, B2038 and B2026 to Chartwell. The A25 and A21 will lead to Knole House, then follow the A21, turning on to the B2027. Hever Castle is a turn off to the left at Bough Beech. The A264 will lead to Tunbridge Wells.

Leith Hill Tower.

❶ Leith Hill

This hill to the south of Dorking, at 938 feet above sea level, is notable as the highest spot in Surrey. The stroll up the hill takes you through beautiful woodland. Tea and cakes are served from the folly at the top of the hill, Leith Hill Tower, where you can rest and enjoy the view.

❷ Chartwell

English wartime prime minister Winston Churchill lived in this Tudor mansion from 1924 until 1965. The house has been preserved by the National Trust in his honour, and includes Churchill's fine collection of art and other personal effects.

❸ Knole House

This extravagant early 17th-century house was commissioned by the Earl of Dorset, Thomas Sackvilles and the rooms are furnished with Sackville family memorabilia, including priceless rugs and tapestries. State rooms include a King's Room and a magnificent ballroom.

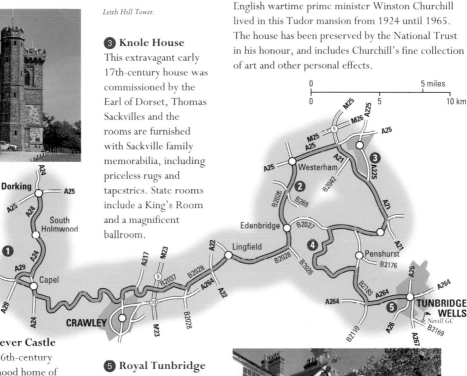

❹ Hever Castle

The 16th-century childhood home of Anne Boleyn, Henry VIII's second wife, was restored in the early 20th century to its Tudor glory by the American millionaires the Astors. The castle grounds are lovingly tended and as are much an attraction as the building itself.

❺ Royal Tunbridge Wells

The heyday of this spa town was in the 18th century, when high society would come here to take the restorative waters. Spring water can still be taken in the town's Bath House.

Old colonnaded shopping street in Tunbridge Wells.

Heritage Hotels – Dovedale
The Peveril of The Peak

Dovedale, Nr Ashbourne, Derbyshire DE6 2AW See map page 8 Tel: (0)870 400 8109 Fax: (0)133 535 0507
Regional General Manager: Debbie Johnson E-mail: HeritageHotels_Dovedale.Peveril_of-the-peak@forte-hotels.com

The romantic-sounding Peveril of the Peak was named after one of Sir Walter Scott's novels. Most likely a local rectory in its original incarnation, it has been a hotel for about 100 years. Standing in 11 acres of terraced lawns, rockeries and grounds, it is surrounded by the splendour of the Peak District National Park and the superb walking areas of the White Peak area.

How to get there
The village of Thorpe is just five miles north of Ashbourne on the eastern side of Dovedale. From junction 25 of the M1 follow the A52 for approximately 30 miles.

Facilities: 46 bedrooms, 2 four-posters, room service, restaurant, bar, lounge, free car park.
Family: baby listening, baby-sitting.

Attractions: Chatsworth. Haddon Hall near Bakewell (the town where the famous pudding is made to a secret recipe). Alton Towers. Good for fishing. Pheasants and wildlife in the garden. Peak Practice was filmed here.

Special Break rates
April–October
£176 per person for 2 nights
November–March
£156 per person for 2 nights
(Excludes 23–26 December and 30 December–2 January 2000)

Special Break
Enjoy a 2-night stay at the Peveril of the Peak Hotel in Dovedale. The Hotel is situated at the edge of the Peak District National Park and is an ideal location to visit Alton Towers, Chatsworth House and Haddon Hall.

On arrival in your room you will be welcomed with a posy of flowers and a box of Thornton's chocolates.

Day 1 – Explore the Blue John Cave and visit the gift shop. Upon your return enjoy a cream tea in the Chatsworth Lounge

Day 2 – Hire a bicycle for the whole day and take in the beautiful countryside on the Tissington Trail. The hotel will arrange for the bicycle to be delivered to the hotel and will also provide you with a hearty packed lunch for your day out.

What's included in your break:
- free entry to the Treak Cliff Cavern (home of Blue John Stone)
- free cycle hire for the whole day and delivery to the hotel
- Thornton's chocolates and flowers in your room on arrival
- 3-course dinner each evening
- full English breakfast each morning
- afternoon tea – day one
- packed lunch – day two

Dovedale

DRIVING ROUTE
The A523 leads from Dovedale to Leek, from where the A53 leads southward to Stoke-on-Trent. Take the A521 and B5471 eastwards to the village of Oakmoor, where Alton Towers will be signposted on B5032. Take the B5030 to Uttoxeter and join the A50 and A511 to Burton-upon-Trent.

Stepping stones across the River Dove, in the Peak District.

① Peak District
The Peak District was England's first national park, established in 1951. The southern half of the park is the more aesthetic area, with limestone hills, wooded dales and pretty villages.

② Leek
Nicknamed "Queen of the Moorlands" for its location on the edge of the Peak District, Leek came to fame as the centre of a silk industry. Nearby is the 18th-century Brindley Mill, built by the same engineer who masterminded the Bridgewater Canal.

③ Stoke-on-Trent
The name Stoke-on-Trent will forever be associated with the beautiful English pottery that was produced here from the end of the 18th century. Great names of the china industry, such as Royal Doulton and Wedgwood are still based here, and the small museum in the town recounts the history and offers examples for sale.

④ Alton Towers
Britain's largest and most popular theme park is set in the heart of Staffordshire. Unlike many other British theme parks, which tend to have a gentle, "fun" approach, Alton Towers prides itself on terrifying rides, such as the Corkscrew and Nemesis.

⑤ Burton-upon-Trent
British beer has many roots in this small town on the River Trent, and the Bass Brewery Museum tells its story, taking visitors through the brewing processes and offering much-needed tastings at the end of the tour.

Potteries museum at Stoke-on-Trent.

53

Heritage Hotels – Dunster

The Luttrell Arms

32–36 High Street, Dunster, Somerset TA24 6SG See map page 3 Tel: (0)870 400 8110 Fax: (0)164 382 1567
Regional General Manager: Brian Shanahan E-mail: HeritageHotels_Dunster.Luttrell_Arms@forte-hotels.com

This is the perfect place for people looking to escape the harshness of present-day reality. Here is a quiet, sleepy village (boasting one main street) in a perfect time warp. When dusk falls over this small 15th-century hotel, even the most prosaic guest might conjure up those medieval times when the Abbots of Cleeve used the Luttrell Arms as a guesthouse. And even insomniacs drift into easy slumber in their four-poster beds amid this kind of tranquillity.

How to get there

The A39 North Devon coast road is the main route to Dunster. Turn south towards Tiverton on the A396. This is the Steep, which becomes the High Street. The hotel is on the left-hand side.

Facilities: 27 bedrooms, 4 four-posters, room service, hairdryer, trouser press, 2 restaurants, bar, lounge, open fires in winter, garden, pay car park.
Family: baby listening, baby-sitting.

Attractions: Elevated gardens entered by walking upstairs. Dunster Castle. Walking. Exmoor for magnificent moorland. Lorna Doone was set in this area.

Special Break 1 rates

3-night (mid-week) break. May–September 1999, £175 per person

Special Break 2 rates

3-night (mid-week) break. November 99–February 2000, £150 per person (Excludes 23–26 December and 30 December–2 January 2000)

Special Break 1

Arrive, check in and enjoy a welcome of champagne and chocolates and a book on Dunster Castle. Savour dinner each evening accompanied with complimentary house wine.

Tickets to visit Dunster Castle are also included and a light bar lunch on one day of your stay.

What's included in your break:
- champagne and chocolates in your room on arrival
- 3 nights' accommodation
- English breakfast
- 3-course dinner every night (½ bottle of house wine per person included every day)
- a book on Dunster Castle
- entrance ticket to Dunster Castle

Special Break 2

Arrive, check in and enjoy a cream tea at your leisure. A pre-dinner drink of your choice is included together with a bottle of house wine with dinner each night. A light lunch or cream tea will also be provided on the other days of your stay.

What's included in your break:
- 3 nights' accommodation
- English breakfast
- 3-course dinner every night (1 bottle of house wine per couple included every day)
- a pre-dinner drink of your choice

Dunster

DRIVING ROUTE

From Dunster the A396 leads into Exmoor National Park. At Wheddon Cross, take the B3224 then the B3190 to reach Tropiquaria at Washford. Take the A358 at Williton and turn left at Crowcombe, driving northeast to Nether Stowey, where Coleridge Cottage is located. Take the A39 to Minehead for the start of the South West Way.

❶ Dunster Castle

The small village of Dunster was the site of a Norman fortress, which operated as a military stronghold until the 17th century. The castle's interior has been restored to emulate its heyday, including a grand banqueting hall and bedrooms.

Just one of the many captivating views from Exmoor National Park. Exmoor has been dramatically affected by centuries of human activities but still supports a diverse range of flora and fauna.

❷ Exmoor National Park

One of the more popular ways to explore this wilderness area is on horse-back, and various riding stables dot the landscape. Walking routes and classically English villages such as Winsford are further attractions. The area is also home to some rare wildlife, including the indigenous red deer.

Bridgwater Bay

The pretty town of Minehead is the start of the South West Way.

❸ Tropiquaria

This tropical animal museum concentrates on the type of reptiles and spiders most people are squeamish about, but it is generally crowded with tourists who want to stroke and hold the creatures. A puppet show and an adventure playground also feature to entertain younger children.

❹ Coleridge Cottage

The poet Samuel Taylor Coleridge lived in this small cottage from 1796 in the small village of Nether Stowey, where he wrote his classic *Kubla Khan* and *The Rime of the Ancient Mariner*. The house preserves the poet's study and living room as they were during his lifetime.

❺ South West Way

Beginning at Minehead, this 600-mile footpath follows the coast of Devon, Cornwall and into Dorset. Along the route, various historical sights, spectacular views and indigenous wildlife delight the hordes of walkers who take to the path every summer.

Heritage Hotels – Exeter
The Southgate

Southernhay, East Exeter, Devon EX1 1QF See map page 3 Tel: (0)870 400 8333 Fax: (0)139 241 3549
Regional General Manager: Brian Shanahan E-mail: HeritageHotels_Exeter.Southgate@forte-hotels.com

Exeter is an ancient, 12th-century Cathedral city and the Southgate, standing next to the Cathedral, succeeds in graciously blending the old and the new. This is a modern hotel, designed in Georgian style, built around the remaining four walls of a listed building. Sir Anthony Hopkins, who filmed *The Remains of the Day* at the nearby Powderham Castle, stayed here and enjoyed the hotel's sports facilities of indoor pool, gym and sauna.

How to get there
Leave the M5 at junction 30, take the 3rd exit (Exeter and Dawlish). Take the 2nd left (signposted to the city centre) and the 3rd exit at the next roundabout. The Southgate is two miles further on at the end of the road.

Facilities: 105 bedrooms, 5 suites, 24-hour room service, mini-bar, hairdryer, trouser press, satellite TV, Cloisters Restaurant, bar, lounge, leisure club, including indoor pool, gym, saunas, solarium, whirlpool bath, free car park.
Family: baby listening, baby-sitting.

Attractions: Fine walking. Nearby Exeter and the Devon coast, Dartmoor and Exmoor. Powderham Castle.

Special Break rates
Minimum stay of 3 nights –
weekends only
May–October 1999, £195 pp
November 1999–March 2000,
£165 pp
(Excludes 22–28 August,
23–26 December and 30
December–2 January 2000)

Special Break
Arrive at your leisure on Friday afternoon, settle into your room, come down and enjoy a traditional Devon cream tea in the lounge.

After breakfast on Saturday discover Exeter's heritage and enjoy a guided walking tour of medieval Exeter. Spend the afternoon exploring Exeter's big-name department stores and speciality boutiques. After all the activity during the day relax over dinner in Cloisters Restaurant and enjoy a complimentary bottle of house wine per couple with your dinner.

On Sunday enjoy a trip north to Exmoor and the quaint village of Dunster, where lunch is provided at the 15th-century Luttrell Arms Hotel. Return to the Southgate Hotel in time for a rest or a refreshing dip in the pool before dinner in Cloisters Restaurant.

What's included in your break:
- 3 nights' accommodation
- traditional Devon cream tea (day 1)
- English breakfast
- guided walking tour of medieval Exeter
- 3-course dinner in the Cloisters Restaurant (a bottle of house wine per couple included one day)
- Sunday lunch at the Luttrell Arms Hotel in Dunster
- access to the pool

Exeter

DRIVING ROUTE

From Exeter drive northwest to Killerton, then continue northwest to the A396 to reach Tiverton. The A361 passes under the M5 to join the A38 towards Taunton – Sheppy's Cider Farm is two miles outside town. From Taunton take the B3170 down to the A303/30. Follow the B3180 towards Exmouth, and A la Ronde is located outside the town, on the A376.

❶ Exeter

Exeter was a major city from its earliest days, first as a Roman settlement, then as a Norman trading centre. Statues in the cathedral commemorate early monarchs, such as Alfred and Richard II. Other medieval buildings abound in the city, including the 14th-century Guildhall. The Quayside area has been renovated into an attractive setting for bars and restaurants.

❷ Killerton House

This 18th-century former home of the Acland family is now the headquarters of the National Trust, which, needless to say, has preserved this building along with many others to reflect its history and heyday.

❺ A la Ronde

This unusual folly is all the more rare for having been designed by two women, Jane and Mary Parminter, at the end of the 18th century. The sixteen sides of the house is only one of its quirks – inside is a staircase covered in shells.

The quayside of the River Exe at Exeter has been transformed into a lively bar and restaurant area.

Be sure to take time out in your trip to enjoy an English cream tea.

❸ Tiverton Castle

First built during the 12th century, Tiverton was largely rebuilt in the 14th century, hence its numerous medieval features. Today the castle has attractions such as secret passage tours, and medieval armour to try on.

❹ Sheppy's Cider Farm

Somerset is the home of English cider brewing, and Sheppy's is a popular tourist stop to see the acres of apple orchards and sample the cider, which has been made here for centuries.

Heritage Hotels – Farnham
The Bush Hotel

The Borough, Farnham, Surrey GU9 7NN See map page 4 Tel: (0)870 400 8225 Fax: (0)125 273 3530
Regional General Manager: James Stewart E-mail: HeritageHotels_Farnham.Bush_Hotel@forte-hotels.com

How to get there
The Bush Hotel is at the lower end of Castle Street where it meets the A325 trunk route.

Facilities: 65 bedrooms, 1 four-poster, 3 mini suites, hairdryer, trouser press, restaurant, bar, lounge, free car park.
Family: baby listening, baby-sitting.

A favourite haunt for guests of this original 17th-century coaching inn is the candlelit, oak-beamed Coachman's Bar, where a log fire crackles in a centuries-old fireplace. In fine weather guests make for the courtyard patio, with its tables perched on ancient cobblestones. The Georgian-style Thackery Restaurant serves traditional English dishes and the lounge features atmospheric frescoes depicting historical scenes with – a rare oddity this – a sundial believed to reflect from the pond in the garden to tell the time. The Bush is mentioned in Thackeray's novel *The Virginians*.

Attractions: Showplace of historic old town is Farnham Castle. Great antique shopping. Losely House. Candon Park. Sutton Place. Birdworld Sanctuary for amateur ornithologists. Frensham Ponds for lakes and walking. Murder Mystery Weekends.

Special Break rates
Weekends only, plus any 2 nights 21 July–30 August 1999
£150 per person for two nights (based on two people sharing)
(Excludes 23–26 December and 30 December–2 January 2000)

Special Break
Arrive at the Bush Hotel at your leisure in the afternoon. Check in to your room and enjoy a cream tea in the fabulous lounge. A 3-course dinner awaits you in Thackery's Restaurant.

Following breakfast, make your way to Wisley Gardens and enjoy a gentle, or not so gentle, walk around the extensive grounds owned by the Royal Horticultural Society.

After such an enjoyable day, Thackery's Restaurant is again the setting for your evening dinner. After a good night's sleep, breakfast is served before your departure. On your way home

stop at Birdworld at Farnham to see the many exotic birds together with the many other attractions at this venue.

What's included in your break:
• 2 nights' dinner, bed and breakfast
• champagne and flowers in your room on arrival
• 3-course dinner in the restaurant each night
• full English breakfast both days
• entry to Wisley Gardens
• entry to Birdworld
• afternoon tea on arrival

Farnham

DRIVING ROUTE

Birdworld is one mile out of town on the A325.
From Farnham the A31 leads directly to Chawton,
where Jane Austen's house is signposted. From here
take the B3006, A3 and B2131 to Haslemere, and the
A283 leads south to Petworth House. Goodwood is
signposted off the A285, which then joins the A272
and leads into Chichester.

Chichester Cathedral.

④ Goodwood

Goodwood House, like
so many English stately
homes, is a cornucopia
of memorabilia
collected by its owners
over the last two
centuries, including
18th-century French
furniture and an art
collection that includes
Van Dyck and
Canaletto. Nearby is
Goodwood racecourse,
which includes a
popular motor-racing
circuit.

⑤ Chichester

Starting life as a Roman
market town,
Chichester was elevated
to the status of a city
with the construction of
its splendid, tall-spired
cathedral in the 12th
century. Its stained
glass and tapestries are
notable features.
Chichester is also
known today for its arts
festival each July, which
is centred round a
programme of plays.

① Birdworld

One of the Britain's
many wildlife reserves,
Birdworld houses many
exotic species of birds,
as well as exotic flowers
in its beautiful gardens.

③ Petworth House

This grand 17th-
century stately home is
best known for its art
collection, which
includes works by the
English artists Turner
and Gainsborough. The
beautiful grounds were
landscaped by the
master gardener
"Capability" Brown.

② Chawton

Towards the end of her
life, the English novelist
Jane Austen lived in this
house and wrote two of
her greatest works,
Pride and Prejudice and
Sense and Sensibility
here. The house
contains many of her
belongings, including
valuable
first editions.

Jane Austen's house at Chawton.

59

Heritage Hotels – Grasmere
The Swan

Grasmere, Nr Ambleside, Cumbria LA22 9RF See map page 10 Tel: (0)870 400 8132 Fax: (0)153 943 5741
Regional General Manager: Colin Campbell E-mail: HeritageHotels_Grasmere.Swan@forte-hotels.com

A close neighbour of Dove Cottage, the Swan is a charming, old-fashioned hotel that prides itself on a true English welcome. Log fires burn in inglenook fireplaces – while in summer the hotel is an ideal base for an exploration of the Lakes.

Attractions: Dove Cottage – Wordsworth's haven. Spectacular countryside. Ideal spot for walking, sailing, horse-back riding, trekking, golfing and motorized biking (quadbiking) into the hills. Rydal Mount.

How to get there
The Swan sits on the northern outskirts of the village of Grasmere, approximately halfway between Windermere and Keswick on the A591. Junctions 36 or 40 of the M6 provide access points.

Facilities: 36 bedrooms, 1 four-poster, 1 half-tester, hairdryer, trouser press, restaurant, 2 bars, lounge, open fires in winter, free car park.
Family: baby listening.

Wordsworth and the Lakes Break rates

Price per person for two nights
May–October 1999
Fri/Sat–£190
Sun/Thur–£165
November 1999–April 2000
Fri/Sat–£180
Sun/Thur–£145
(Excludes 23–26 December and 30 December–2 January 2000)

Wordsworth and the Lakes Break

Situated on the outskirts of the village of Grasmere, this charming inn nestles in the most spectacular scenery imaginable.

Most bedrooms offer panoramic views of the fells through the Vale of Grasmere.

In your room on arrival champagne and Grasmere's famous gingerbread will be waiting.

Dinner in the Waggoner Restaurant features the best of traditional cooking and reflects the awards gained in recent years.

After breakfast you have the choice of visiting either Dove Cottage or Rydal Mount. Dove Cottage was William Wordsworth's home for nine years and next door is the museum, which illustrates the poet's life with manuscripts, portraits and memorabilia.

Rydal Mount was the poet's home for 37 years and retains a lived-in family atmosphere with few changes and includes a four-acre garden much as he designed it.

After lunch an "eight lakes tour" is arranged, which takes you over Dunmail rise to Keswick and on to explore Borrowdale, Buttermere and Newlands valleys. Ascend both the dramatic Honister Pass as well as Newlands Hause. You will be driven alongside Derwent Water, Buttermere and see Crummock Water, before returning along the quiet west side of Thirlmere.

Dinner will again be four courses in the charming and hospitable environment that brings guests back time and again.

Breakfast prior to departure, with a last chance to explore before your journey home.

What's included in your break:
- 2 nights' dinner, bed and breakfast (wine not included)
- champagne and gingerbread
- tour of north lakes scenery
- entry to Dove Cottage and museum or Rydal Mount

Grasmere

DRIVING ROUTE

Rydal and Grasmere both lie on the A591. Proceed north along this road to Keswick, and take the B5289 around Derwent Water to the A66, leading to Cockermouth.

Derwent water in autumn.

① Rydal

One of William Wordsworth's homes in the region was Rydal Mount, and the house, including the poet's study, has now been turned into a museum, documenting his life and work. The surrounding area in Rydal, like most of the Lake District, is stunning.

② Dove Cottage

Wordsworth's most famous Lake District home was in Grasmere itself. Here he wrote some of his finest work, as well as an early guidebook to the region he loved. A tour around Dove Cottage includes views of his original poetry manuscripts.

④ Keswick

This 13th-century town made its name for its production of graphite, which was used as lead in pencils until the 18th century. Also near the town is a mysterious stone circle, reminiscent of Stonehenge.

③ Derwent Water

One of many lakes from which the region takes its name is Derwent Water, and the nearby village of Borrowdale is one of the most attractive in the area. Lake cruises are available to take in the beautiful views.

Rydal Fell. The surrounding area was the home and the inspiration of one of England's greatest poets, William Wordsworth.

⑤ Cockermouth

The birthplace of William Wordsworth continues the tradition of its neighbouring towns by commemorating their greatest son. Wordsworth House is now a museum.

Heritage Hotels – Helmsley

The Black Swan

Market Place, Helmsley, North Yorkshire YO62 5BJ See map page 11 Tel: (0)870 400 8112 Fax: (0)143 977 0174
Regional General Manager: Gavin Dron E-mail: HeritageHotels_Helmsley.BlackSwan@forte-hotels.com

The face of this small, 45-room hotel is a blend of Elizabethan, Georgian and Tudor – all of it charming with warm, welcoming interiors of candlelight, oak beams and open fireplaces. Revelling in the friendly, family atmosphere, two members of staff have been serving in the Rutland Room Restaurant for a joint total of 97 years. You don't find staff like that any more!

Attractions: Gateway to the North Yorkshire Moors. Glimpses of TV series Heartbeat *folk filming in this area. Castle Howard, setting for the TV series* Brideshead Revisited, *which was filmed here. Duncombe Park. Fine-quality shopping. York 27 miles away.*

How to get there

Helmsley is 15 miles to the east of Thirsk on the A170 in the direction of Scarborough. Sutton Bank, just before Helmsley, offers the driver a true test of skill, and, reassuringly, caravans have now been forbidden from attempting this route.

Facilities: 45 bedrooms, 1 half-tester, hairdryer, restaurant, 2 bars, lounge, open fires in winter, free car park.
Family: baby listening.

Special Break rates

£220 per person for weekends (Friday and Saturday night)
£180 per person for mid-week stays
Available June 1999–October 1999

Special Break

Arrive on your chosen day and settle into your room, which provides you with all the comforts you would expect from this well-appointed hotel. A bottle of champagne on ice will be delivered to your room, providing you with the ideal excuse to relax and read the complimentary copy of the history of the Black Swan and the surrounding areas of Helmsley.

As evening comes enjoy a full choice from the menu in the Rutland Room Restaurant, followed by coffee in one of the five lounges.

In the morning you will be provided with complimentary tickets to visit Castle Howard, home to the Howard family and the location used for the filming of *Brideshead Revisited*. In order that your day is uninterrupted you will also be given a packed lunch to enjoy at your leisure. You may choose to spend the full day exploring the stately home and its gardens or visit some of the many other places of interest that are mentioned within the Black Swan book.

On your second evening enjoy once again a full choice from the menu with time to reflect on all you have seen during the day.

The following morning there is no need to rush off. If possible you can check out late, giving you a last chance to walk around the town and buy some of the more unusual items that may not normally be available to you. Perhaps you may even be tempted to stay for lunch by the offer of two lunches for the price of one prior to your departure.

What's included in your break:
- 2 nights' dinner, bed and breakfast
- a bottle of champagne in your room on arrival
- a copy of the history of the Black Swan and the surrounding areas of Helmsley
- 2 dinners in the Rutland Room Restaurant (wine not included)
- a packed lunch (day 2)
- entrance tickets to Castle Howard

Helmsley

DRIVING ROUTE

Rievaulx Abbey is three miles outside Helmsley on the B1257. Return to Helmsley and take the A170 east – Hutton-le-Hole is signposted to your left. Continue along the A170 to Pickering, then Scarborough. Take the A64 through Malton to reach Castle Howard. The B1257 will lead back to Helmsley.

❷ Hutton-le-Hole

One of the most attractive villages in the north, Hutton-le-Hole continually buzzes with tourists, but nowhere else is there such a fine example of everyday Yorkshire moorland village life.

❶ Rievaulx Abbey

This 12th-century Cistercian abbey was the centre of a thriving community in its heyday, but its walls were destroyed in the 16th century and it is now in ruins. The nearby terraces make for wonderful views.

The majestic Castle Howard.

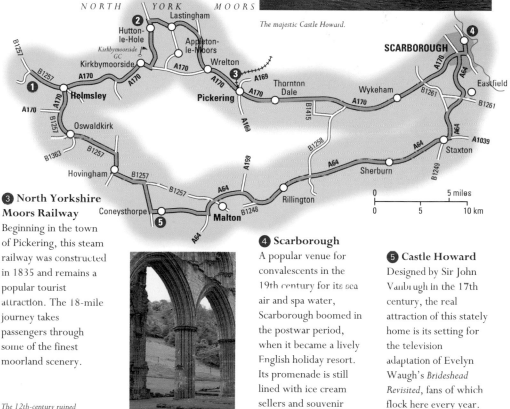

❸ North Yorkshire Moors Railway

Beginning in the town of Pickering, this steam railway was constructed in 1835 and remains a popular tourist attraction. The 18-mile journey takes passengers through some of the finest moorland scenery.

The 12th-century ruined Cistercian abbey at Rievaulx.

❹ Scarborough

A popular venue for convalescents in the 19th century for its sea air and spa water, Scarborough boomed in the postwar period, when it became a lively English holiday resort. Its promenade is still lined with ice cream sellers and souvenir shops in summer.

❺ Castle Howard

Designed by Sir John Vanbrugh in the 17th century, the real attraction of this stately home is its setting for the television adaptation of Evelyn Waugh's *Brideshead Revisited*, fans of which flock here every year.

Why spend every weekend in the same garden?
We have over 200 to choose from.

Discover over 200 different gardens with the National Trust. From rose gardens to kitchen gardens, landscape to water gardens, woodland and orchards, every season holds its own surprises.
For a free copy of the National Trust's gardens map guide, please call +44 (0)171 447 6700, Monday-Friday 9.30 am-5.30 pm quoting ref.H1.

The National Trust,
36 Queen Anne's Gate, London SW1H 9AS.
E-mail: traveltrade@ntrust.org.uk
Web Site: www.nationaltrust.org.uk

THE NATIONAL TRUST

Where history *never* repeats itself

CHAPEL DOWN

WORLD CLASS WINES FROM ENGLAND

Chapel Down wines produce England's finest range of wines. Grapes grown in well tended vineyards across the south England are made into a diverse selection of styles by international winemaker David Cowderoy at their winery located at Tenterden Vineyard Park in the beautiful county of Kent – The Garden of England

Chapel Down's Epoch 1 dry red and oak style Epoch V white wine

Grapes have been grown in England for centuries right back to Roman times. Throughout the medieval period vines continued to flourish. However, England was well established as a trading nation and with the crown's association with Bordeaux, the foreign wines became more common place. Prior to the modern revival English viticulture tended to confine itself to the aristocracy. Although in Samual Pepys' diaries he records drinking wines from vineyards located around the City of London.

It was not until the 1950's that English vineyards once again became commercial enterprises. Today the country can boast 1000 hectares of vineyards, primarily planted in the south eastern part of the country. Well chosen vineyard sites with south facing slopes, protection from wind and frost and well drained soils will yield delicately flavoured grapes that are suitable for wine making. The harvest normally takes place in October after the grapes have had the benefit of our usually warm September weather, which gives the vines an extra boost late in the season.

Chapel Down wines have been praised for their quality and style both in the United Kingdom and overseas. you can now enjoy them at Heritage Hotels across the country.

Heritage Hotels – Hereford
The Green Dragon

Broad Street, Hereford HR4 9BG See map page 7 Tel: (0)870 400 8113 Fax: (0)143 235 2139
Regional General Manager: James Lever E-mail: HeritageHotels_Hereford.Green_Dragon@forte-hotels.com

The Green Dragon hostelry was already old when they were seeking planning permission for the city's magnificent cathedral, home of the medieval *Mappa Mundi*. Spick and span villages of black and white houses and churches look as though they were built yesterday. For those seeking mental sustenance there is Hay-on-Wye, the second-hand book capital of the world, and for the inner man, there are regular appearances on the Green Dragon's restaurant menu of such delights as Wye Valley salmon, Herefordshire hop cheese and Herefordshire beef.

How to get there
The Green Dragon sits right in the centre of Hereford, on Broad Street, north-west of the cathedral.

Facilities: 48 bedrooms, 2 four-posters, 3 suites, hairdryer, trouser press, restaurant, bar, lounge, free car park.
Family: baby listening, babysitting

Attractions: May Fair. Also May: 3-day 100-mile raft race down the Wye from Hay to Chepstow. Annual Festival of Arts in July. The Wye Valley. Black Mountains.

Special Break rates
April–October
Mid-week/Weekend
£150
November–March
Mid-week/Weekend
£150
Prices are per person for two nights including the activities mentioned.
(Excludes 22–28 August, 23–26 December and 30 December–2 January 2000)

Special Break
Visit the Green Dragon Hotel set in the beautiful city of Hereford. Arrive any time after 2pm and check in to your room. Once you have settled in and relaxed take afternoon tea in the Carrick Lounge, followed by a stroll around the historic cathedral and view the famous Map of Mundi.

Arrive back and freshen up before dinner is served in the lovely Shires Restaurant with its original oak-panelled walls. After dinner take coffee in the Carrick Lounge with a complimentary liqueur coffee.

After a leisurely breakfast, there is much to see in this lovely county so why not visit one of the two following attractions: Dinmore Manor with its unusual herbaceous shrubs and pines; alternatively visit the Cider Museum and Distillery. Return to the hotel for a Herefordshire cream tea served in the lounge. Prior to your 3-course dinner visit the Cocktail Lounge for a complimentary aperitif of your choice.

Following breakfast the next day be sure to collect your complimentary bottle of apple aperitif brewed exclusively at the Offer Distillery and conclude your visit with some shopping in the city centre prior to departing.

What's included in your break:
• 2 nights' dinner, bed and breakfast
• afternoon tea
• 3-course dinner with coffee (wine not included)
• complimentary pre-dinner cocktail
• complimentary liqueur coffee
• entrance to Dinmore Museum or the Cider Museum and Distillery
• a bottle of apple aperitif brewed at the Offer Distillery

Hereford

DRIVING ROUTE

The A49 leads directly north from Hereford to Leominster. From here, take the A44 and the A4110 to Croft Castle. Take the B4361 to reach Ludlow, then take the A4113 east to Knighton, and join the B4357 and B4594 south to Hay-on-Wye. From here, follow the B4352 back to Hereford.

❶ Hereford Cathedral

This wonderful cathedral, built in stages between the 13th and 16th centuries, is best known for possession of the *Mappa Mundi*. This large parchment map was drawn up in 1289, and, uniquely for its time, shows the artist's idea of the world, placing Jerusalem at its centre. It remains the finest cartographic treasure in the world.

Hereford Castle in the snow.

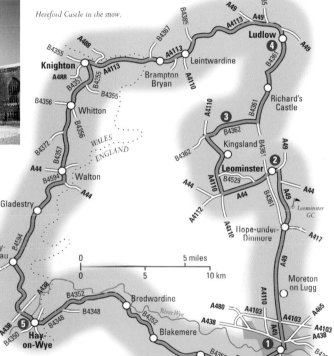

❷ Leominster

This pretty medieval town, lined with antiques shops, makes for a pleasant stop-off. One of the more unusual features is the traditional ducking stool, where thieves and conmen – and occasionally, adulterers – were punished by being doused in water.

❸ Croft Castle

A cacophony of styles graces this castle, first built in the 14th century, and developed by various owners over the years. Gothic, Georgian and Regency are among the architectural innovations employed here. The gardens preserve numerous avenues of trees.

❹ Ludlow

More than 400 buildings in this pretty town have been listed by the National Trust for their architectural value, including Ludlow Castle, built in the 11th century. Today it houses a spectacular open air theatre.

❺ Hay-on-Wye

The annual Literary Festival is held in this small Welsh town in May, attracting renowned authors from around the world. The rest of the year visitors can lose themselves in the innumerable second-hand bookshops.

Tudor house in Ludlow. The town boasts more than 400 listed buildings.

Heritage Hotels ~ Hertingfordbury
The White Horse

Hertingfordbury, Herts SG14 2LB See map page 5 Tel: (0)870 400 8114 Fax: (0)199 255 0809
Regional General Manager: Frank Harvey E-mail: HeritageHotels_Hertingfordbury.White_Horse@forte-hotels.com

The Georgian façade of the White Horse actually belies a much older interior with oak beams dating back 400 years. Many of the spacious bedrooms overlook the hotel gardens, where lunch, drinks and a truly English tea are served in summer. In the grounds of nearby Hatfield House is the Old Palace, where Elizabeth I spent her childhood and learnt of her accession to the throne. The Old Palace is today the setting for regular Elizabethan banquets, providing insights into the lifestyle of the rich and famous centuries ago.

How to get there
Take the A414 to Hertingfordbury and on reaching the village turn into Hertingfordbury Road. The hotel is on the right.

Facilities: 42 bedrooms, restaurant, bar, lounge, free car park.
Family: baby listening, baby-sitting.

Attractions:
Cambridge. Hertford Castle. Bramfield Forest. St Alban's Cathedral. Knebworth House. 14th-century village church. The valley of the River Mimram. Lea Valley Park with 23 miles of sport and entertainment.

Special Break rates
January–June, October–November, £110 per person for two nights (based on two sharing) (Excludes 23–26 December and 30 December–2 January 2000)

Special Break
The White Horse, steeped in history and tradition and surrounded by countryside, is an ideal base to combine good food and comfortable surroundings with a visit to the Imperial War Museum, one of Britain's top aircraft and military museum attractions.

Arrive and settle in before tucking into an afternoon cream tea in the lounge or, weather permitting, the delightful garden.

Enjoy a relaxing 3-course dinner with coffee in the Conservatory Restaurant served with a complimentary bottle of red or white Chilean wine and round off the evening in the comfort of the lounge.

Come down to a leisurely breakfast before setting off to Duxford, Europe's premier aviation museum featuring the award-winning American Air Museum.

Return and unwind with an aperitif in the bar before again enjoying dinner in the Conservatory Restaurant.

Following breakfast, why not visit the Mosquito Aircraft Museum, a short drive from the hotel, before driving home.

What's included in your break:
- 2 nights' dinner, bed and breakfast
- a complimentary bottle of Chilean red or white wine between two each evening
- afternoon cream tea on the day of arrival
- entry to the Imperial War Museum Duxford (except on Airshow days)

Hertingfordbury

DRIVING ROUTE
The B158 leads into Hertford from Hertingfordbury, then take the A414 to Hatfield. Join the A1 and exit at junction 6 onto the B656 to Knebworth. Continue along this road to Hitchin, then take the A505 to Royston. Wimpole Hall lies north along the A1198. The B1046 leads into Cambridge. The A10 will lead back south to Hertingfordbury.

❶ Hertford Castle
The administrative town for the county of Hertfordshire is dominated by its Norman Castle, dating from the Norman Conquest of 1066. Another charm of the town is the many antique shops, which line its traditional streets.

❷ Hatfield House
This Tudor mansion has a rich royal history, most notably as the house in which Elizabeth I was "held hostage" by her half-sister Mary. The house thrives on its link with the Virgin Queen and includes many pieces of personal memorabilia within its richly decorated rooms.

Be sure to hire a punt and cruise past the beautiful grounds of the Colleges whilst in Cambridge.

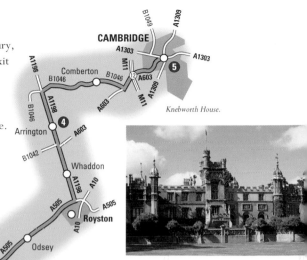

Knebworth House.

❸ Knebworth
Many of the artefacts on display in this Tudor house are souvenirs from India, reminiscent of the fact that one-time owner Lord Lytton was the first Viceroy during the great days of the British Empire. Today the house is best known for the large-scale rock concerts held in its vast grounds.

❹ Wimpole Hall
This imposing mansion dates from the 18th century, but various renovations have taken place since, leaving the house a conglomeration of architectural styles. The servants' quarters remain original, and a fascinating insight into life "downstairs".

❺ Cambridge
Like Oxford (*see page 90*), the main reason to visit this eastern town is for its ancient university buildings, but Cambridge tends to be quieter and less touristed than its slightly older counterpart. One of the most beautiful sights is the King's College Chapel, with its 16th-century interior and its famed boy's choir, which performs each evening. Also like Oxford, the river plays a vital part in Cambridge life, and riverside pubs abound along the Cam's banks.

Heritage Hotels – Kingston

Kingston Lodge

Kingston Hill, Kingston-Upon-Thames KT2 7NP See map page 4 Tel: (0)870 400 8115 Fax: (0)181 547 1013
Regional General Manager: Ben Godon E-Mail: HeritageHotels_Kingston_upon_Thames.Kingston_Lodge@forte-hotels.com

The name has been deeply embedded in the history of the area for four centuries. It stands on the edge of one of London's greatest areas of greenery, Richmond Park, which has more than 2400 acres of woodland parkland in which to ramble and perhaps share a quiet shady spot with a herd of Royal deer. The Lodge's bedrooms – one of which holds a four-poster bed – overlook Coombe Wood golf course or the flowers in the hotel courtyard. The Burnt Orange Restaurant offers an international selection of dishes.

Attractions: Rugby at Twickenham. Tennis at Wimbledon. Horse-racing at Sandown Park. Hampton Court Palace. Kew Gardens nearby. Wisley Royal Horticultural Society Gardens.

How to get there
Kingston Lodge sits up on Kingston Hill barely five minutes from the Robin Hood roundabout on the A3.

Facilities: 64 bedrooms, 1 four-poster, 2 mini suites, hairdryer and trouser press in all bedrooms, restaurant, bar, lounge and free car parking.
Family: baby-sitting on request.

Special Break rates
Validity dates: 1 June 1999–31 March 2000
June–September 1999
£142 per person
October–December 1999
£122 per person
January–March 2000
£122 per person
(based on two people sharing)
Single supplement £20 per person per night.
(Excludes 23–26 December and 30 December–2 January)

Special Break
Day 1 – Arrive at your leisure, check in to one of the recently refurbished rooms, and enjoy dinner in the Mediterranean surroundings of the Burnt Orange Restaurant overlooking The Courtyard Garden.

Day 2 – After breakfast, you are invited to visit Hampton Court with the hotel's compliments. This is England's finest royal palace, with over 500 years of history, and is situated on the banks of the River Thames. Follow in the footsteps of some of the greatest kings and queens through the magnificent state apartments, Great Hall and Chapel Royal.

In the afternoon, a visit to Ham House at Petersham is recommended. An outstanding Stuart House built in 1610, Ham is famous for its lavish interiors and spectacular collections of fine furniture, textiles and paintings, as well as for the 17th-century formal gardens.

Return to the hotel to relax with an aperitif in the lounge and reflect over dinner on the wonders of the day.

Day 3 – After a hearty English breakfast, checking out of the hotel, and before you leave for home, wander round London's greatest park, Richmond Park. This 2400-acre parkland was created in 1637 by Charles I. Formal gardens blend with parkland where up to 700 fallow deer wander free. There is also Penn Ponds, Isabella Plantation, and an enclosed garden famous for its rhododendrons and azaleas.

What's included in your break:
• 2 nights' dinner, bed and breakfast
• ticket to Hampton Court (open every day except 24th–26th December. Mid-March to mid-October 9.30am to 6pm. Last admission 45 minutes before closing – normal ticket entry price £10 adult, £7.60 senior citizen)
• 3-course table d'hôte dinner menu (with coffee included)

Kingston

DRIVING ROUTE

The A307 from Kingston leads to Richmond, from where it is a short drive to Kew. The A205 and A316 lead to Chiswick. Return on these roads and go east to Putney; the A219 leads south to Wimbledon. Return to Kingston along the A238, and Hampton Court is one mile west of the town along the A308.

Tropical plants in the hothouse at Kew Gardens.

① Richmond upon Thames

The favoured home of the Tudor royal family, little remains of the former Richmond Palace, but the presence of royalty secured the position of this elegant town. The river lends it most of its character, the area around the bridge (London's oldest) buzzing with restaurants and bars. The vast Richmond Park, inhabited by deer, is another prime attraction.

② Royal Botanical Gardens

These 18th-century gardens are one of outer London's main tourist attractions. Most famous is the glass building of the Palm House in which various tropical plants thrive.

③ Chiswick House

Based on the designs of Italian architect Andrea Palladio, Chiswick House and its beautifully landscaped gardens were the centre of artistic society in the 18th century, entertained by the owner, the Earl of Burlington.

④ Wimbledon

The world's most famous tennis championship takes place in the Wimbledon Lawn Tennis Club for two weeks each June. It is known as much for the rain that stops play and for the servings of strawberries and cream as it is for the tennis.

⑤ Hampton Court Palace

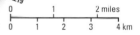

Home to Henry VIII and then Elizabeth I, Hampton Court is the finest Tudor palace in the country. The interior preserves the ornate state rooms, private apartments and works of art, as well as the 16th-century kitchens. The grounds include a maze, ever crowded with lost and confused tourists.

The ornate Hampton Court Palace and Gardens.

Heritage Hotels – Lavenham
The Swan

High Street, Lavenham, Sudbury CO10 9QA See map page 5 Tel: (0)870 400 8116 Fax: (0)178 724 8286
Regional General Manager: Elizabeth Combridge E-mail: HeritageHotels_Lavenham.Swan@forte-hotels.com

How to get there
The main A1141, off the A134 Sudbury to Bury St Edmunds road, runs into Lavenham itself and the Swan is located on the main High Street.

Facilities: 41 bedrooms, 3 four-posters, 2 suites, 24-hour room service, hairdryer, trouser press, restaurant, 2 bars, 5 lounges, open fires in winter, free car park.
Family: baby listening, baby-sitting on request.

History lives on in every groan and creak of the floorboards in this ancient picturesque inn, which rates as one of East Anglia's most glorious treasures, while Lavenham is regarded as the best-preserved and most unspoilt Tudor village in Britain. The restaurant, with a period minstrel's gallery, serves traditional dishes. The Garden Bar was a favourite for US army air corps based here in WWII and retired soldiers still visit. Bandleader Glenn Miller is said to have had a drink here before his last fateful flight. Cream teas are to be found in the gardens, served beneath parasols.

Attractions: Gainsborough House. Long Melford, and a mile-long road of fine shopping, notably antiques. Ikworth House, National Trust property with glorious grounds. Bury St Edmunds Cathedral. Gateway to Constable country.

Special Break rates
November 1999–March 2000
£90 per person, per night (weekends)
£85 per person, per night. (mid-week).
(Excludes 23–26 December and 30 December–2 January 2000)

Feature rooms, four-posters and suites are available for a small supplementary charge

Special Break
Lavenham is one of England's best-preserved medieval villages, situated in the beautiful countryside of Suffolk.

The Swan Hotel is found in the centre of the village and is renowned internationally for its excellent customer service and fine dining.

Lavenham is the perfect base for exploring the University City of Cambridge, Colchester, England's oldest town, or Bury St Edmunds, famous for its abbey and gardens. Alternatively you may visit Kentwell Hall, Ikworth House, Melford Hall and Audley End.

Why not visit the Swan for a unique experience and enjoy a romantic stay?

Upon arrival enjoy a complimentary fruit punch while you register, then relax in the comfort of your room, which will be supplied with chocolates, flowers and bathrobes.

Before dinner, there is the chance to experience the history of Lavenham via an audio walking tour from the front of the hotel. Upon your return, enjoy a pre-dinner drink prior to your meal in the restaurant, accompanied by the resident pianist.

The following day, enjoy a leisurely breakfast before touring the area. In addition to the destinations already mentioned, to be recommended is a trip around "Lovejoy Country", including numerous antique shops, or reminisce at Flatford Mill or Dedham, where John Constable painted his famous landscapes.

Upon your return, quench your thirst and appetite in the lovely surroundings before you again return to the comfort of your room.

After breakfast, spend a few moments in the spacious gardens and capture your memories on a postcard to your friends and relations before you begin your journey home.

What's included in your break:
• 2 nights' accommodation including house dinner and breakfast (wine not included)
• chocolates and flowers in the room upon arrival
• welcome glass of fruit punch
• audio tour of Lavenham

Lavenham

DRIVING ROUTE

Kentwell Hall lies on the A134, close to the village of Lavenham. The road then leads south to Sudbury. Continue on the A134, then take the B1068 and B1070 southeast to Flatford Mill. The A137 leads into Colchester.

① Lavenham

In the 15th century, England's wool trade was largely based in this village, and the residents have since carefully preserved its Tudor atmosphere. Buildings such as the Guildhall form part of what seems a "living museum".

② Kentwell Hall

The current owner of this 16th-century mansion has lovingly restored it to is original glory, and takes visitors through life in Tudor times, complete with staff in authentic costumes speaking in archaic Tudor language. For anyone with an interest in this rich period of history, it should not be missed.

This crooked house forms part of the "living museum" of Lavenham

③ Sudbury

Two major artistic talents put this otherwise unassuming town on the map. In the 18th century it was the birthplace of the great English painter Thomas Gainsborough, and his house has been preserved as a museum. The author Charles Dickens used Sudbury as the fictional setting for his humourous novel, *Pickwick Papers*.

④ Flatford Mill

This small house was the site from which the region's finest artist, John Constable, painted his most famous work, *The Hay Wain*. Nearby Bridge Cottage is now a museum devoted to the artist and his landscapes of English country life in the 19th century.

The painter Thomas Gainsborough (1727–88), depicted here in a self-portrait (painted 1759), was born in the town of Sudbury.

⑤ Colchester

Generally considered to be England's oldest town and its first capital, as well as the site of one of Queen Boadicea's rampages. The original Roman walls of the town can still be seen. The Norman castle is also worth a visit, particularly for its museum on the town's history.

Heritage Hotels – Lincoln
The White Hart

Bailgate, Lincoln LN1 3AR See map page 8 Tel: (0)870 400 8117 Fax: (0)152 253 1798
Regional General Manager: Gavin Dron E-mail: HeritageHotels_Lincoln.White_Hart@forte-hotels.com

At the heart of the medieval city of Lincoln lies the White Hart, facing the overwhelming splendour of the ancient cathedral. The quaint cobbled streets leading up to the hotel, which was endowed with its emblem by Richard II when he stayed at the hostelry in 1372, are reminiscent of earlier centuries. There are mellow interiors with a fine collection of antique furnishings and, in the lounge, a collection of Rockingham china. Traditional English dishes are served in the King Richard Restaurant and the informal Orangerie Bistro.

How to get there
The White Hart is located in Bailgate, mid-way between the castle and the cathedral. The towers of the cathedral make a good landmark for new arrivals.

Facilities: 48 bedrooms, 12 suites, hairdryer, trouser press, 2 restaurants, bar, lounge, open fires in winter, free car park.
Family: baby listening, baby-sitting.

Attractions: The cathedral, which art critic John Ruskin eulogised as "the most precious piece of architecture in the British Isles". Lincoln Castle. Ellis' Mill. Incredibly Fantastic Old Toy Show (Toy Museum). The Lawn conservatory with tropical plants. Museum of Lincolnshire Life.

Special Break rates
£155 per person per night
Validity date: Until 31 March 2000
This offer is subject to availability with only a limited amount of rooms each day being allocated at this rate. Double or twin room for single occupancy carries a supplement from £20 per night
(Excludes 23–26 December and 30 December–2 January 2000)

Special Break
Enjoy a relaxing two-night stay at the White Hart in the heart of the medieval city of Lincoln.
Not only will you be offered two nights' dinner, accommodation and breakfast, also included are many added extras to enhance your stay and make your visit to Lincoln into one you will always wish to remember.

What's included in your break:
• 2 nights' dinner, accommodation and breakfast
• upgrade to the best room available upon check in

• luxury Lincolnshire bedroom package to include hand-crafted chocolates, a bottle of champagne and Lincolnshire plum bread
• entry into 3 of the city's main attractions – the Usher Gallery with its unique collection of paintings by local artists, miniatures, ceramics and glassware; Lincoln Castle, home of the few surviving copies of the Magna Carta; and Lincolnshire Life Museum, which houses the Tritton Tank (the first known fighting tank), designed in the Yarborough Room at the White Hart Hotel

Lincoln

DRIVING ROUTE

Take the B1190 out of Lincoln to Horncastle, and travel south along the B1192 to Tattershall Castle, which is off the A153. The B1192 joins the A1121 to Boston. Back along the A1121, join the A17 to Heckington. Continue along this road towards Sleaford, and take the A15 and A153 to Ancaster. Belton House is southwest of here. The A607 will lead you northward back to Lincoln.

The magnificent medieval Tattershall Castle.

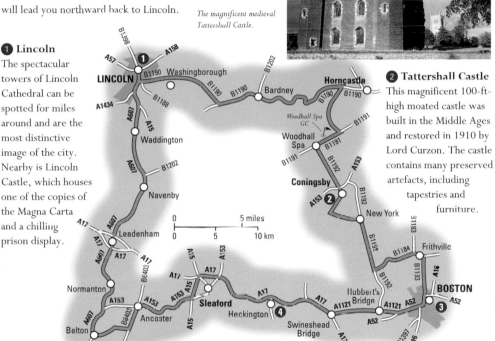

❶ Lincoln

The spectacular towers of Lincoln Cathedral can be spotted for miles around and are the most distinctive image of the city. Nearby is Lincoln Castle, which houses one of the copies of the Magna Carta and a chilling prison display.

❷ Tattershall Castle

This magnificent 100-ft-high moated castle was built in the Middle Ages and restored in 1910 by Lord Curzon. The castle contains many preserved artefacts, including tapestries and furniture.

The Heckington eight-sail windmill is claimed to be the only working one of its type in England.

❸ Boston

The familiar name of this attractive Anglo-Saxon town stems from the fact that the Pilgrim Fathers were arrested and imprisoned here when trying to escape to Holland. When they finally reached the New World, they named a new settlement after this Lincolnshire town.

❹ Heckington Windmill

Built in 1830, this eight-sailed windmill is still a working flour mill, grinding the corn solely by wind power. Flour made at the mill is on sale at the windmill shop.

❺ Belton House

This grand, late 17th-century house was built for a family of aristocrats who used their fortune to elaborately decorate their home, including some intricate limewood carvings. Family portraits by artists such as Reynolds line the walls.

Heritage Hotels – Marlborough
The Castle & Ball

High Street, Marlborough, Wilts SN8 1LZ See map page 4 Tel: (0)870 400 8118 Fax: (0)1672 51 5895
Regional General Manager: Adam Terpening E-mail: HeritageHotels_Marlborough.Castle_and_Ball@forte-hotels.com

Marlborough is a town of Jacobean, Georgian and even medieval houses, and the Castle and Ball fits beautifully into this ancient environment. It was once a coaching inn from the 15th century and some of its surviving oak timbers pre-date the Spanish Armada. They pass through much of the front of the hotel and its bedrooms, among them the Summerfield, with its own balcony overlooking the High Street. The restaurant, Manton's, is split-level with – a decadent touch – a silk-tented ceiling.

How to get there
Both the A338 and A4 lead into Marlborough and eventually into the High Street. The Castle and Ball is in the centre of town on the High Street.

Facilities: 34 bedrooms, 1 four-poster, hairdryer, trouser press, bar, restaurant, lounge, open fires in winter, free car park.
Family: baby-sitting can be arranged.

Attractions: Wildlife-rich Savernake Forest. Boat trips on the Kennet and Avon Canal. Lamborn and the valley of racehorses. Racing: the classic Hennessy Gold Cup at Newbury racecourse in November. Mop Fairs (funfairs) in October. Avebury, ancient remains. Stonehenge.

Special Break rates
Leisure break price
Validity date: July 99–March 2000
(Excludes 23–26 December and 30 December–2 January 2000)

Special Break
For a minimum of 2 nights during July and August, the package includes a complimentary visit to the Devizes Museum.
The museum traces the history of the Wiltshire landscape, and boasts one of the finest prehistoric collections in Europe, rivalling that of the British Museum, with finds from Avebury and West Kennett.

Marlborough

The purpose of these standing stones at Avebury is still unclear.

DRIVING ROUTE

From Marlborough follow the A4 westward, where the Avebury Stone Circle will be signposted to your left. The A361 southward will take you to the town of Devizes. Rejoin the A361 and then follow the A365 and the A350 to Lacock. Corsham Court is a couple of miles northwest from here, off the A4. Continuing northwest, join the B4039 to reach Badminton.

❶ Avebury Stone Circle

Similar to Stonehenge, this ancient stone circle is thought to date from 2500 BC. The purpose of this huge circle marked out by stones is not known, although historians tend to assume it was a religious site.

❷ Devizes

The museum in the centre of this old market town is the prime attraction, with its detailed information on many archaeological finds from prehistoric times discovered throughout England. Anyone with an interest in ancient history should visit here.

❸ Lacock

Considered one of the most beautiful villages in England, Lacock is somewhat crowded and commercialised, but its authenticity makes it well worth a visit. A museum dedicated to resident Fox Talbot, the first Englishman to make a photograph negative, is located in the village.

The abbey at Lacock.

❹ Corsham Court

John "Beau" Nash and "Capability" Brown were responsible for the renovations on this Elizabethan manor, whose revered art collection includes works by Michelangelo.

❺ Badminton

This small village is largely known for its annual horse trials, a major feature on the equestrian calendar and frequented by royalty.

Heritage Hotels – Marlow
The Compleat Angler

Marlow Bridge, Marlow, Bucks SL7 1RG See map page 4 Tel: (0)870 400 8100 Fax: (0)162 848 6388
Regional General Manager: Caroline Bellenger E-mail: HeritageHotels_ Marlow.Compleat_Angler@forte-hotels.com

Smooth, lush lawns sloping down to the banks of the Thames form an idyllic setting for this picturesque hotel with a spectacular view of the Marlow Weir. The original 400-year-old bar still serves as a cosy drinking den, with open fires on chilly days. Take tea with freshly baked scones, preserves and clotted cream beneath garden parasols.

Attractions: Champagne picnicking on the river. Croquet on the lawn. Fly fishing. Fine shopping in Marlow, predominantly clothes and china. Marlow regatta in June. Other high-society events in the area: Ascot in June and Henley in July.

How to get there
The A404 dual carriageway links the M4 and M40 motorways. At the first roundabout follow signs for Bisham – the hotel is on the right immediately before Marlow Bridge.

Facilities: 65 bedrooms, 2 suites, 5 four-posters, 24-hour room service, hairdryer, trouser press, satellite TV, the Riverside Restaurant, the Mange 2 Brasserie, bar, lounge, open fires in winter, croquet, riverbank fishing, summer boat trips, tennis court, gym (within walking distance), boat moorings, free car park.

Wine and Boating Weekend rates
Validity dates:
16–18 July,
20 July–1 August
10–12 September
£259 per person per night
£25 single person supplement

A Taste of the Thames Weekend rates
Validity dates:
9–11 and 22–24 October
5–7 and 19–21 November
£259 per person per night
£25 single supplement

Wine and Boating Weekend
Starting with a welcome cocktail party, enjoy a weekend of gourmet food, fine wines and some "messing about on the river".

Highlights of the weekend include a visit to the Old Luxters Vineyard on the slopes of Hambledon Valley for an exclusive tasting of their Chiltern Valley Wines, and the opportunity to explore one of the most beautiful stretches of the River Thames on a river cruise from the hotel's private jetty.

What's included in your break:
- 2 nights' accommodation
- cocktail reception
- 3-course dinners with half-bottle of wine
  (2 nights)
- English breakfast
- afternoon tea (Sat)
- visit to the Old Luxters Vineyard
- river cruise
(Transport to the vineyard and the river cruise are also included)

A Taste of the Thames Weekend
A taste of the Thames. After a welcome cocktail party explore life on the Thames from Isaak Walton to the present day: gourmet food, fine wines and the river's allure.

Visit historic Henley on Thames and the "River and Rowing" Museum to experience the Regatta in its Edwardian heyday with all its regalia and even a full-sized steam launch. Meander along the banks of the river and enjoy a taste of England with full-bodied Chiltern Valley Wines from the Old Luxter Vineyard on the slopes of Hambledon Valley.

What's included in your break:
- 2 nights' accommodation
- cocktail reception and introductory talk
- 3-course dinner with half-bottle of wine
  (2 nights)
- English breakfast
- afternoon tea (Saturday)
(Transport and entrance to the museum and the vineyard are included)

Marlow

DRIVING ROUTE

From Marlow take the A4155 and the A4094;
Cliveden is on your left, Cookham on your right.
Then journey on the A4 to Maidenhead. Henley is to
the west of Maidenhead, along the A404 and A4130.
Follow this road until the turn off on to the B480 to
reach Stonor Park.

❸ Maidenhead

This pretty town on the
banks of the Thames,
with fine views of
Windsor, was a busy
coaching stop during
the 18th century for
travellers to and from
London, although the
nearby woods were rife
with highwaymen.

❹ Henley-on-Thames

Prettily located on the
Thames, with a famous
bridge built in 1786,
Henley is dominated by
the 13th-century St
Mary's Church with
its 16th-century flint
tower. One of
England's many grand
occasions is the Henley
Royal Regatta, a rowing
competition that takes
place at the end of
June.

❶ Cliveden

Once home to Nancy
Astor, Britain's first
female member of
Parliament, the house
was a hub of political
social gatherings in the
1930s. In the 1960s,
the house was the
setting for risqué
parties, which launched
the Profumo affair
scandal involving the
beautiful Christine
Keeler.

❷ Cookham

An attractive town
on the banks of the
Thames, Cookham is
also known as the home
of eccentric religious
artist Stanley Spencer,
who adapted many
biblical tales to the
surroundings of his
native village. The
town's chapel displays
some of his work.

The River Thames at Maidenhead.

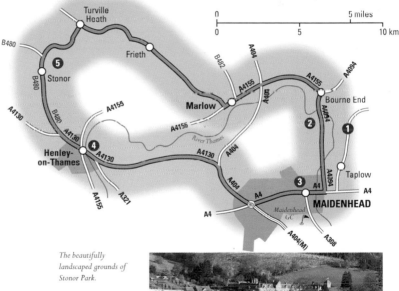

The beautifully landscaped grounds of Stonor Park.

❺ Stonor Park

Although most of this ancestral home dates from the
14th century, with later additions to the façade, there
is evidence that a smaller house existed here as early
as 1190. Sir Edmund Campion used the house as a
refuge while writing his *Decem Rationes*, and Stonor
now includes an exhibition about his life.

79

Liberty hand embroidered, organza scarf. Regent Street, London WIR 6AH. Telephone: 0171 734 1234.

LIBERTY

the art of the IDIOSYNCRATIC.

Champagne POMMERY.
Ordinary days can have extraordinary moments !

Heritage Hotels – Matlock Bath

The New Bath Hotel

New Bath Road, Matlock, Bath DE4 3PX See map page 8 Tel: (0)870 400 8119 Fax: (0)162 958 0268
Regional General Manager: Debbie Johnson E-mail: HeritageHotels_Bath.Matlock.New_Bath@forte-hotels.com

Matlock Bath first became recognised in Regency times for its medicinal springs. The New Bath Hotel was built in 1802 and boasts an outdoor pool and an indoor heated plunge pool both fed by natural springs. The old mining area has become a tourist attraction and the Heights of Abraham is popular for the cable car that runs high above the town to Victoria Tower and the mining shafts.

How to get there

From the M1 leave at junction 28. Follow the signs to Matlock along the A38. Turn off at the A610 and follow signs to Ambergate. Turn right at the A6 towards Matlock. The hotel is on the left-hand side just before you reach Matlock Bath.

Facilities: 55 bedrooms, 8 half-testers, 2 four-posters, hairdryer, trouser press, restaurant, bar, lounge, open fires in winter, tennis court, Leisure Club includes thermal-fed indoor heated plunge pool, sauna, solarium, thermal-fed outdoor pool, free car park.
Family: baby listening, baby-sitting, children's play area.

Attractions: Croquet. Indoor plunge pool. Sailing, regattas, golf and junior putting green. Antiques Gallery. Peak District National Park. Chatsworth House. Haddon Hall. Alton Towers. Carsington Reservoir. Good shopping in nearby Matlock.

Pottery and Bone China Break rates

April–October
£155 per person for 2 days
November–March
£135 per person for 2 days
(Excludes 23–26 December and 30 December–2 January 2000)

Pottery and Bone China Break

On arrival in your room you will find a complimentary box of Thornton's chocolates and a posy of flowers.

A tour and demonstration is offered around the museum and factory shop at the celebrated Royal Crown Derby Centre.

Also included is a fully guided tour of the Derby Pottery Visitors Centre

Upon your return each day you will be able to enjoy a cream tea in the Spinners Lounge at your leisure.

What's included in your break:
- entry to the Royal Crown Derby Centre
- entry to the Denby Pottery Visitors Centre
- Thornton's chocolates and flowers in your room on arrival
- 3-course dinner each evening
- full English breakfast each morning
- afternoon tea each day

Matlock Bath

DRIVING ROUTE

The A6 leads to Haddon Hall, then directly on to Bakewell and Buxton. Follow the road north to Chapel-en-le-Frith, then take the A625 to Edale and the start of the Pennine Way. Continue on this road past Hope, then return south on the B6049 and A623 to Chatsworth House on the B6012. The A6 leads back to Matlock Bath.

Chatsworth House in autumn.

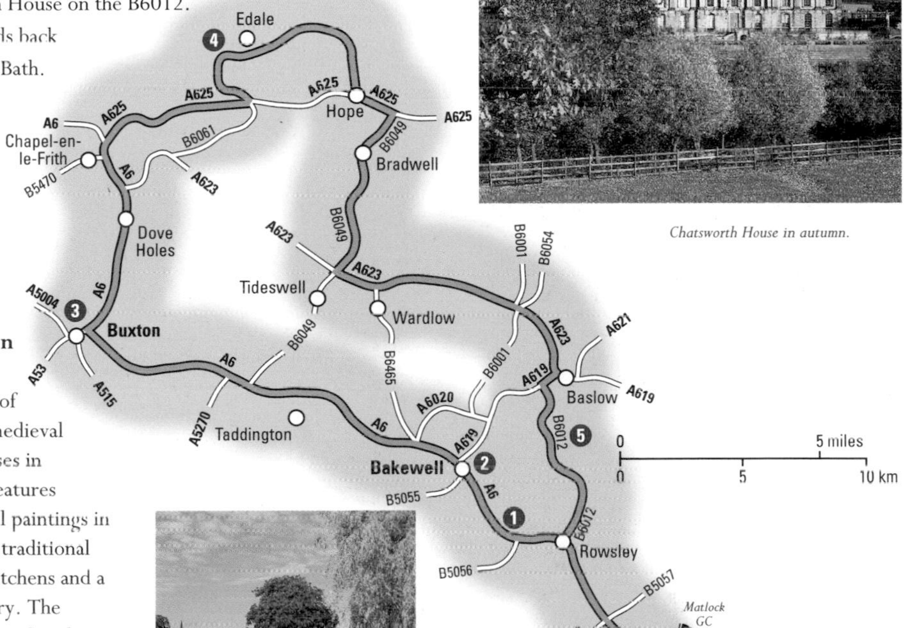

❶ Haddon Hall

This is one of the finest medieval manor houses in England. Features include wall paintings in the chapel, traditional medieval kitchens and a Long Gallery. The house was used as the location of Rochester's home in the film adaptation of *Jane Eyre*.

The River Wye at Bakewell.

❷ Bakewell

This attractive town on the River Wye is home to the traditional Bakewell Pudding, a sweet almond pie misnamed as the Bakewell Tart. The pie is still made here, much to visitors' delight, who purchase it in huge quantities.

❸ Buxton

The Romans were the first to discover the fresh spring water of this Derbyshire town, which is now bottled and exported around the world. The Regency architecture in Buxton is a result of the 18th-century passion for spa towns.

❹ Pennine Way

The 250-mile route that extends to Scotland begins at Edale in the north Peak District. The full walk takes about three weeks to complete, but visitors turn up all year route to walk just a part of the wilderness route.

❺ Chatsworth House

The traditional home of the Duke of Devonshire was built in the 17th century. A highlight of the interior is the elaborate dining room, where the table setting is exactly as it was for the visiting King George V in 1933. The spectacular gardens were designed by "Capability" Brown.

Heritage Hotels – Mudeford

The Avonmouth Hotel

Mudeford, Christchurch, Dorset BH23 3NT See map page 4 Tel: (0)870 400 8120 Fax: (0)120 247 9004
Regional General Manager: Adam Terpening E-mail: HeritageHotels_Mudeford_Christchurch.Avonmouth@forte-hotels.com

The hotel, built in the 1820s, is set in extensive grounds with stunning views of the Christchurch estuary, Mudeford Quay and the dramatic Hengistbury Head. A recent addition to the hotel is the Orchard Wing, situated near the water's edge. Various sailing craft are available and the marshes and mudflats here offer promising exploration. The coastline is rich in conservation areas and wildlife sanctuaries. Ferry over to Hengistbury Head or simply loll around the hotel grounds, before enjoying dinner in the Harbour View Restaurant.

How to get there
Take the M27 to junction 1 and then the A35 to Christchurch. Follow the ample signs for Mudeford and you will find the hotel situated in the centre of the village.

Facilities: 40 bedrooms (14 located in separate ground-floor wing with estuary views), room service, hairdryer, trouser press, restaurant and bar overlooking the estuary, 2 lounges (1 non-smoking), heated outdoor swimming pool (June–August), croquet lawn, junior putting green, free car park.
Family: baby listening, baby-sitting, games room (July–August).

Special Break rates
Validity dates: 1 November 1999–31 March 2000 (Excludes 23–26 December and 30 December–2 January 2000)

Special Break
Whatever the weather, a day at the Poole Pottery is a wonderful experience, where you can not only enjoy a tour of the factory but also pick up some real bargains.
What's included in your break:
• a visit to Poole pottery
• complimentary gift of Poole pottery as a lasting memory of your stay at the hotel

Attractions: Croquet on the lawn. Swimming pool. Wildlife sanctuaries. Sailing. Golf. Leisure Centre. Isle of Wight. Bournemouth. New Forest.

Mudeford

DRIVING ROUTE
The A35 leads westward from Mudeford to
Bournemouth. Then go north along the A3049/341
to reach Wimborne Minster. Kingston Lacy is a
further two miles along the B3082. From here go to
Poole along the A350, then join the A35/351 to reach
Corfe Castle. Durdle Door can be reached westward
through the coastal villages, at the end of the B3071.

*The unusual rock formation of
Durdle Door.*

❶ Bournemouth

A 19th-century
creation, this seaside
town is largely known
now as a haven for
retired people, but
benefits from an
abundance of parkland.
The Romantic poet
Shelley lived in the
suburbs of the town,
and a museum holds
personal belongings of
him and his wife, Mary
Shelley, authoress of
Frankenstein.

❷ Wimborne
Minster

The town is named in
honour of its ancient
and impressive church,
which has numerous
Norman details. The
church's library is one
of the oldest in the
country, dating from
1686.

*The town of Corfe Castle, which
takes its name from the ruined
castle on the hill behind.*

❸ Kingston Lacy

A 17th-century stately
home, worth visiting,
like many of its
counterparts, for its art
collection, including
works by Rubens.
Another room houses
souvenirs from the
19th-century travels of
the home's then owner,
William Bankes.

❹ Corfe Castle

This ancient castle
suffered cruelly at
the hands of the
Roundheads during the
English Civil War. They
ousted the Royalist
Bankes family, who
then moved to Kingston
Lacy. Reduced to ruins
by the attack, the castle
remains a popular
visitor attraction.

❺ Durdle Door

One of southern
England's most
photographed sights is
this limestone arch
jutting out from the
bay. Nearby is another
tourist hotspot, the
semicircular Lulworth
Cove.

Heritage Hotels – North Berwick
The Marine

Cromwell Road, North Berwick, East Lothian HE39 4LZ See map page 13 Tel: (0)870 400 8129 Fax: (0)162 089 4480
Regional General Manager: Joe Longmuir E-mail: HeritageHotels_Berwick.Marine@forte-hotels.com

The Marine Hotel is a gloriously embellished example of Victoriana, picturesquely located at the heart of East Lothian's golfing coast. The Marine actually overlooks the 16th green of North Berwick's championship West Links course, which threads along the edge of the Firth of Forth and includes one of golf's most-copied holes, the infamous 15th "Redan". Real golf afficionados should take one of the 40 sea view rooms and suites at the rear, where they can watch players tackling several holes of the West Links course from dawn to dusk.

How to get there
From the A198, Dirleton Avenue, turn into Hamilton Road and take the second right into Cromwell Road.

Facilities: 83 bedrooms including 6 four-posters, 5 suites and 4 mini suites, hairdryer, trouser press, restaurant, bar, lounge, Leisure Club includes heated outdoor pool (May–October), sauna, solarium, table-tennis, 2 tennis courts, putting green, snooker, gardens, hairdresser, free car park.
Family: baby listening, children's playground, nursery.

Special Break rates
£20 per person per night extra
Validity date: any day from June 1999–March 2000 (Excludes 23–26 December and 30 December–2 January 2000)

Special Break
Our Golf Inclusive Break offers a Welcome Golf Pack, 3 balls and a towel plus one round of golf per day at the Whitekirk golf course for only an extra £20 per person per day. Situated 3 miles east of North Berwick, the course has commanding views over East Lothian and beyond. Hosting the televised Professional MasterCard East Lothian Classic in 1998 put Whitekirk on the map – and the Classic will be returning again in 1999. Whitekirk also has an excellent 300-yard practice range.

What's included in your break:
• a Welcome Golf Pack, 3 balls and a towel
• a round of golf per day at the Whitekirk golf course.

Attractions: Bass Rock and its colony or gannets, Fidra Island, inspiration for Treasure Island, seascape across the Firth to the hills of Fife, medieval castle ruins, Lammermuir Hills, tennis courts, rose garden, swimming pool, putting greens. North Berwick is one of the driest parts of Britain.

North Berwick

DRIVING ROUTE

Tantallon Castle lies to the east of North Berwick on the A198, and has views of Bass Rock, which can be reached by ferry from North Berwick. Take the B1345, B1377 and A6137 south to Haddington, then the A1 west to Edinburgh. Hopetoun House is to the west of Edinburgh, on the A90/904.

① Tantallon Castle

This ruined castle is best known for its striking and windswept position on the edge of a cliff. It was the home of the Scottish Douglases, until it succumbed to war in 1651.

③ Haddington

Traditionally a farming town, the appeal of Haddington today lies in its 17th- and 18th-century houses, whose architectural features include ornamental gables and towers.

④ Edinburgh

The capital of Scotland is an attractive city built on an extinct volcano and with a rich past. One of the most popular sights is the castle on top of the mound, which dates from the 12th century. The city is always busy, but it is crammed to bursting twice a year – during the popular arts festival in August and for Scotland's lively Hogmanay celebrations each New Year's Eve.

Firework celebrations at the Edinburgh festival.

② Bass Rock

A ferry from North Berwick takes visitor to this island rock, which has now been turned into a bird sanctuary. Gannets, puffins and cormorants are among the species that can be seen here.

⑤ Hopetoun House

The finest stately home in Scotland, Hopetoun House was built in the 18th century in a grand Baroque style. Art and tapestries are on display inside, and the grounds, with their the riverside setting, are a popular resting spot.

The ruined Tantallon Castle is an evocative sight, perched as it is at the edge of a cliff.

Heritage Hotels – Oxford
The Eastgate

The High Street, Oxford OX1 4BE See map page 4 Tel: (0)870 400 8201 Fax: (0)186 579 1681
Regional General Manager: Tony Marrinan E-mail: HeritageHotels_Oxford.Eastgate@forte-hotels.com

Originally a 17th-century coaching inn, the hotel has had recent renovations that remain in keeping with the mellow architecture of the city. It is situated right in the centre of the town and Magdalen College is a near neighbour. Tours of the colleges are easily arranged. In turn, Oxford students have quite taken to the hotel's lively Café Boheme, a French-style brasserie providing jazz in the afternoon. A sister bar, also Bohemian in character, serves coffee and drinks. There's punting on the river and good shopping in Oxford.

How to get there
The Eastgate is situated right in the very heart of central Oxford on the High Street.

Facilities: 63 bedrooms, 1 mini suite with four-poster, 24-hour room service, hairdryer, trouser press, restaurant, bar, lounge, free car park.
Family: Baby listening, babysitting.

Attractions: The colleges; Blenheim Palace; Apollo Theatre; Gateway to the Cotswolds.

Bohemian Oxford Break rates
Validity dates: all dates until March 2000
£140 per person for a 2-night break (based on two people sharing. Wine not included with meals)
(Excludes 23–26 December and 30 December–2 January 2000)

Bohemian Oxford Break
You will arrive at the Eastgate Townhouse, directly opposite the Oxford University Examination Halls.

The new Café Boheme Restaurant is the sister to the Café Boheme in Soho, London. It is a lively restaurant and bar with a mix of students, artists and the local café society. Most evenings live jazz is played and it is a wonderful place to sit and watch Oxford unfold.

You will choose a 3-course meal from the extensive menu and no doubt stay a while to soak up the atmosphere of the bar, which is open until 1am each night.

The next morning, Café Boheme is the setting for breakfast with probably the best cappuccino in town, while reading the newspaper. Entry is organised into the Oxford Story attraction, which transports you through 800 years of the University. This is only a 10-minute walk from the hotel and you can browse in the famous Blackwells Bookstore and all the shops along the way.

A book of discount vouchers for some of the Bicester Village discount retail outlets is included, which offers between 10% and 35% discount on various designer labels (e.g. Racing Green, Versace, Calvin Klein etc.) – 25 minutes' drive from the hotel.

After a good day's shopping you will be ready to hit Café Boheme once again and maybe even the nightlife of Oxford afterwards!

Following breakfast the next morning, before departing you might like to take a tour of one of the colleges or slip back to Bicester Village once again.

What's included in your break:
• 2 nights' accommodation
• 2 dinners in Café Boheme
• 2 breakfasts in Café Boheme
• entry to the Oxford Story
• discount vouchers for Bicester Village

Oxford

DRIVING ROUTE

Head for the A34 ring road to the west of Oxford, then follow the A420 and A338 past Wantage to the B4507 to see the White Horse carved into the hills. A right turn towards Woolstone leads back onto the A420 where, at Faringdon, take a left onto the A417 to Lechlade. A right-hand sign will lead to the village of Kelmscot. Return to the A417 again to Cirencester, from where the B4425 leads to Burford, via Bibury. The busy A40 will lead back into Oxford.

First carved into the chalk hills 4,000 years ago, the purpose of this strange, almost clumsy-looking figure on White Horse Hill remains a mystery.

① White Horse Hill

This 375 ft shape of a horse is thought to have been carved into the chalk hills around 2000BC. Its meaning is unclear, although some believe it to be an ancient form of signposting.

The Market Place and church at Cirencester is the focal point of this ancient Roman city.

② Kelmscot

This Tudor home, near the town of Lechlade, was the summer residence of archetypal English designer William Morris, whose decor is preserved within the house.

③ Cirencester

This ancient Roman city still revolves around its Market Place, which made it a thriving centre of trade for hundreds of years. A 15th-century church decorated with flying buttresses and several 17th- and 18th-century houses make it an attractive place to visit.

④ Bibury

A freshwater trout farm, which includes an extensive breeding programme, is one of the attractions of this small village on the fringe of the Cotswolds.

⑤ Burford

The idyllic setting of this town, on the banks of the river Windrush, is typical of the Cotswolds area. A 15th-century church and a high street lined with antiques shops make it a popular stop for tourists.

89

Heritage Hotels – Oxford
The Randolph

Beaumont Street, Oxford OX1 2LN See map page 4 Tel: (0)870 400 8200 Fax: (0)186 579 2133
Regional General Manager:Tony Marrinan E-mail: HeritageHotels_Oxford.Randolph@forte-hotels.com

Chapters Bar and Fellows' Lounge are popular meeting places often featured on screen (Debra Winger and Anthony Hopkins were there for *Shadowlands*, and TV's *Inspector Morse* is a regular). Plush Victorian burgundy decor and opulent candlelit settings in the Spires Restaurant conspire to make dining a sybaritic experience.

Attractions: An art collection worth a million pounds hangs in the Lancaster room, predominantly quirky paintings by humourist Osbert Lancaster.

Architecture, visits to Oxford colleges, a plethora of bookshops, Oxford's graduate parade, antique shops.

How to get there
Follow signs to the city centre, this leads directly to St Giles. Prominent on the corner, to your right, you will spy the Randolph.

Facilities: 119 bedrooms, 9 suites, 7 mini suites, 5 half-testers, 1 four-poster, 24-hour room service, hairdryer, trouser press, satellite TV, restaurant, bar and bistro, Chapters bar, open fires in winter, car park adjacent (special terms available for hotel guests).
Family: Baby listening, baby-sitting.

Luxury at the Randolph rates
Validity dates: all dates until March 2000 – subject to availability
May–November
£280 per person for two nights
December–April
£255 per person for two nights
Upgrade to suite
£40 per person for two nights
Based on two sharing. Wine not included with meals (Excludes 23–26 December and 30 December–2 January 2000)

Luxury at the Randolph
The dreaming spires of Oxford await you on your two-night break at the world-famous Randolph Hotel.

Right in the heart of the city, the Randolph has been home to royalty, elder statesmen and celebrities and is Oxford's premier hotel.

The hotel is within an easy walk of museums, shops and theatres. Waiting in your room on arrival will be champagne, flowers and chocolates.

Before having your meal in the Spires Restaurant you will enjoy one of Ailish's champagne cocktails in the Chapters Bar, the setting for many *Inspector Morse* novels, then a 3-course meal in the restaurant with coffee and petits fours in Fellows' Lounge.

Enjoy a leisurely breakfast the next day before having a tour of Oxford on the open-topped bus, which will pick you up from right outside the hotel. Entry tickets are arranged to nearby Blenheim Palace (15 minutes' drive), the home of the Duke of Marlborough (available only until the end of October – although the gardens designed by Capability Brown are open throughout the year), followed by afternoon tea at the romantic Bear Hotel at Woodstock.

No doubt you will be ready for another of Ailish's cocktails after all this sightseeing and again the Spires Restaurant is the setting for your evening meal.

After breakfast, before you depart, as a memento of your stay in Oxford, you will be presented with an *Inspector Morse* novel signed by the author Colin Dexter.

What's included in your break:
- 2 nights' dinner, bed and breakfast
- champagne, chocolates and flowers on the first night
- one of Ailish's champagne cocktails each evening before your meal
- a tour of Oxford on the first morning
- entry to Blenheim Palace
- afternoon tea at the Bear in Woodstock
- one copy per couple of a signed *Inspector Morse* novel

Oxford

WALKING ROUTE:

A stroll around Oxford, en route to the major sights, will inevitably bring you within the grounds of numerous university colleges and their striking architecture, from medieval to modern. Oxford is also a busy city with a complicated one-way road system, so exploring is best done on foot, or – to take a lead from the students – on bicycle.

❶ Ashmolean Museum

Britain's oldest public museum was founded in 1683. Among its displays are diverse collections of British, European, Egyptian and Eastern antiquities; European paintings and sculpture; and Indian and Oriental art. Particularly popular are the coins and medals housed in the Heberden Coin Room.

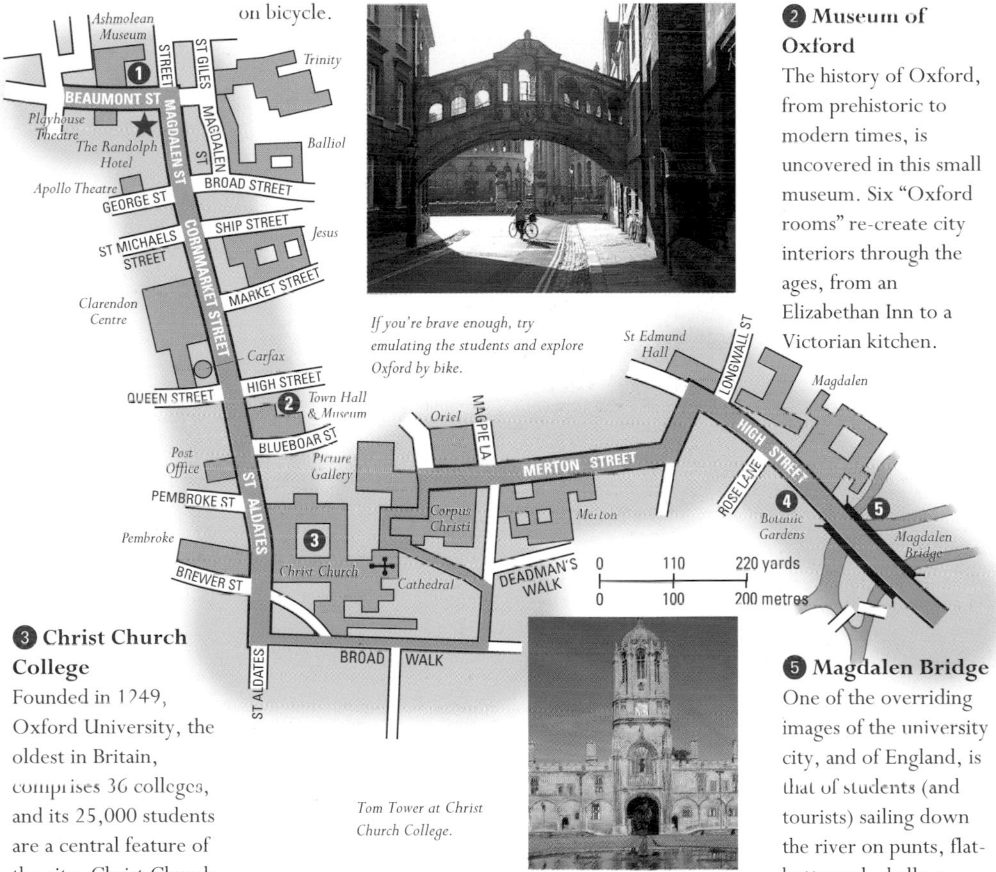

If you're brave enough, try emulating the students and explore Oxford by bike.

❷ Museum of Oxford

The history of Oxford, from prehistoric to modern times, is uncovered in this small museum. Six "Oxford rooms" re-create city interiors through the ages, from an Elizabethan Inn to a Victorian kitchen.

❸ Christ Church College

Founded in 1249, Oxford University, the oldest in Britain, comprises 36 colleges, and its 25,000 students are a central feature of the city. Christ Church college features a 16th-century chapel that serves as the city's cathedral. Many of the other colleges have notable architectural features.

Tom Tower at Christ Church College.

❹ Botanic Gardens

The Botanic Gardens belong to the University of Oxford, and are the oldest such gardens in the country. Created in the early 17th century, the walled gardens contain medicinal herbs as well as a diverse collection of international plants. Glasshouses

❺ Magdalen Bridge

One of the overriding images of the university city, and of England, is that of students (and tourists) sailing down the river on punts, flat-bottomed, shallow-water boats steered with long poles. They can be hired at various points along the river, but the Magdalen Bridge is one of the most popular and central.

91

Heritage Hotels – Padstow
The Metropole

Station Road, Padstow, Cornwall PL28 8DB See map page 2 Tel: (0)870 400 8122 Fax: (0)184 153 2867
Regional General Manager: Brian Shanahan E-mail: HeritageHotels_Padstow.Metropole@forte-hotels.com

Padstow is a paradise for those who love seafood. Its views are pretty spectacular too, particularly from the Metropole, an imposing Victorian hotel, which stands on a hill overlooking the harbour and Camel estuary. Padstow's narrow streets are dotted with small colourful shops and you can find amazing antiques. Or walk along the beaches and find clams.

Attractions: Rick Stein, TV cook (and his restaurant) are here. Numerous small villages in the area. Bedruthan Steps (rock formation). Tintagel and nearby Camelford, setting for Camelot legend. Jamaica Inn, *immortalised by Daphne du Maurier.*

How to get there
Locate the B3890, off the A389 near Wadebridge then follow this road down into the town, around Padstow docks, which are overlooked by the Metropole.

Facilities: 50 bedrooms, 3 four-posters (1 with balcony), 5 mini suites (1 with balcony), restaurant, bar, lounge, heated outdoor pool (July–August), hairdryer, trouser press and free car park.

Special Break 1 rates
3-night (mid-week) break
May–October 1999
£230 per person

Special Break 2 rates
3-night (mid-week) break
November–February
£165 per person
(Excludes 23–26 December and 30 December–2 January 2000)

Special Break 1
Check into your sea view room and a welcome of champagne and chocolates. Enjoy a complimentary aperitif each evening prior to dinner.

Tickets will be provided for you to visit The Lost Gardens of Heligan (May–October) at your leisure. Enjoy a light lunch or cream tea each day in the Sun Terrace overlooking the estuary.

What's included in your break:
- champagne and chocolates in your room on arrival
- 3 nights' accommodation
- English breakfast
- 3-course menu dinner (wine not included)
- aperitif each evening prior to dinner
- tickets to the Lost Gardens of Heligan
- light lunch or cream tea

Special Break 2
Check into your sea view room, then relax in the lounge and enjoy a cream tea. A pre-dinner drink and a bottle of (house) wine with dinner each evening is also included. Enjoy a light lunch or cream tea on each of the other days. Enjoy a complimentary aperitif each evening prior to dinner.

Tickets will be provided for you to visit the Lost Gardens of Heligan (May–October) at your leisure. Enjoy a late lunch or cream tea each day in the Sun Terrace overlooking the estuary.

What's included in your break:
- 3 nights' accommodation
- English breakfast
- 3-course menu dinner (one bottle of house wine per couple included)
- aperitif each evening prior to dinner
- cream tea (day 1)
- light lunch or cream tea (days 2 & 3)

Padstow

The picturesque Polperro harbour and town.

DRIVING ROUTE

Polzeath lies to the north of Padstow, along the A389, A39 and B3314. Continue on the latter route to Tintagel. The B3314 is also the best access route to Bodmin Moor. Then follow the B3254 south to the village of Polperro. The A387 and A390 will lead you to St Austell.

4 Polperro

One of Cornwall's most picturesque villages, which has thrived on its fishing industry, is made all the more romantic with its history of 19th-century smuggling.

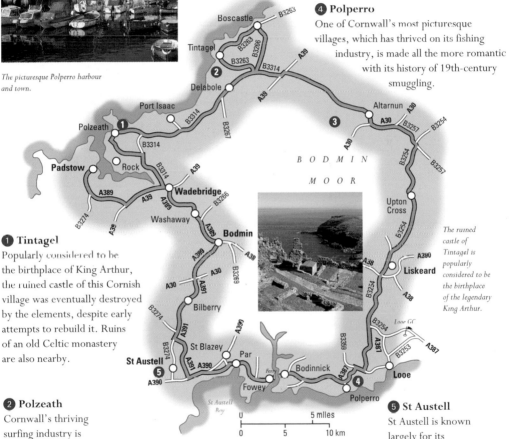

The ruined castle of Tintagel is popularly considered to be the birthplace of the legendary King Arthur.

1 Tintagel

Popularly considered to be the birthplace of King Arthur, the ruined castle of this Cornish village was eventually destroyed by the elements, despite early attempts to rebuild it. Ruins of an old Celtic monastery are also nearby.

2 Polzeath

Cornwall's thriving surfing industry is centred around Polzeath, with its high and ferocious waves. The beaches are regularly dotted with avid contenders, and tuition is offered for beginners.

3 Bodmin Moor

A small but bleak wilderness, Bodmin Moor is dotted with a few picturesque villages but is best known for its setting of Daphne du Maurier's novel *Jamaica Inn* and, in more recent years, for its so-called "Beast of Bodmin", an animal thought to resemble a bear or a panther, which has been spotted roaming the landscape.

5 St Austell

St Austell is known largely for its production of porcelain china, made out of local clay, which was once thought only to exist in the Far East. The industry has thrived since the 18th century.

Heritage Hotels – Romsey/New Forest
The White Horse

Market Place, Romsey, Hampshire SO51 8ZJ See map page 4 Tel: (0)870 400 8123 Fax: (0)179 451 7485
Regional General Manager: Adam Terpening E-mail: HeritageHotels_Romsey.White_Horse@forte-hotels.com

The Regency facade conceals a building that dates in part back to the 14th century. The hotel is a short walk from Broadlands, the 18th-century house where Lord Palmerston, Queen Victoria's Prime Minister, and Lord Mountbatten once lived. Recently come to light inside the ancient hotel – unearthed from beneath five centuries of paint and paper – is a series of Tudor wall paintings decorating various parts of the hostelry. Oak beams are in abundance and traces exist of an Elizabethan mummers' gallery. An old courtyard dating back to its coaching inn days is a popular stop for drinks.

How to get there
After leaving the M27 at junction 3, follow the A3057 to Romsey, then follow signs to the town centre and Market Place. Drive past the hotel and take the first turning left into Latimer Street, which will deliver you into the hotel car park.

Facilities: 33 bedrooms, hairdryer, trouser press, restaurant, bar, lounges, free swimming pool and fitness centre nearby, free car park.
Family: baby listening, baby-sitting.

Attractions: The New Forest nearby with its wild ponies. Stonehenge. Winchester and Salisbury cathedrals. Local leisure facilities: swimming, sauna, squash, tennis, riding and golf course.

Special Break rates
Validity date: July and August 1999
November 1999–March 2000
Leisure break rates
(Excludes 23–26 December and 30 December–2 January 2000)

Special Break
Enjoy a complimentary visit to Broadlands, the home of Lord and Lady Romsey. This superb Palladian mid- Georgian house is about 10 minutes' walk from the hotel and a truly lovely stately home with landscaped gardens by Capability Brown. Previous occupants of Broadlands have included Lord Palmerston and Lord Mountbatten.

What's included in your break:
• visit to Broadlands

From November onwards a free visit to the famous National Motor Museum at Beaulieu in the heart of the New Forest has been arranged. The museum is well known for its collection of cars and motorcycles but is also next door to the Palace House and gardens, which form part of the visit.

What's included in your break:
• ticket entrance to the National Motor Museum at Beaulieu
• ticket entrance to the Palace House and its gardens

Romsey/New Forest

DRIVING ROUTE

Broadlands is situated on the southern outskirts of
Romsey. From here follow the A3090 to the M27; exit
at junction 1 on to the A31 into the New Forest where
you will see the Rufus Stone. Lyndhurst is on the A337,
from where the B3056 leads to Beaulieu.

❶ Romsey Abbey

Romsey Abbey was the site of a Benedictine nunnery
in Norman times, and the grand architecture of the
church is a mark of the respect the order gained from
the community. Oak trees from the New Forest
were used for the roof timbers. In the 16th
century, the people of Romsey bought the
church from the king, and it has since been
Romsey's parish church.

❷ Broadlands

The birthplace of Lord
Palmerston, the mid-
19th-century prime
minister, Broadlands
was also the home
of Lord Louis
Mountbatten. The
Prince and Princess of
Wales spent part of
their honeymoon
in the Georgian
house.

Beaulieu palace and garden

❸ Rufus Stone

In the heart of the New
Forest is this monument
to King William II (also
known as William
Rufus), assassinated
here in 1100. The
murderer is unknown,
but the prime suspect
was William's brother,
who ascended the
throne as King Henry I.

Typical thatched cottage at
Lyndhurst.

❹ Lyndhurst

The central town of the New Forest, Lyndhurst
supplies information about trails and walks in the
area. The town is also the burial site of Alice Liddel,
who as a little girl inspired Lewis Carroll's stories of
Alice in Wonderland.

❺ Beaulieu

This stately home,
standing on the site of a
former abbey, is best
known for its National
Motor Museum, a
collection of 250 motor
vehicles, ranging from
classic cars from the
early days of motoring,
through to the land-
speed racer, the
Bluebird. An exhibition
also explains the history
of automobiles.

Proof that you don't need to be really rich & sweet to be attractive.

Let us introduce you to Glenfiddich Malt Whisky

Liqueur, with its truly smooth taste, that's not too

rich, nor too sweet; a character of irresistible

warmth, which everyone will find instantly desirable.

Glenfiddich
MALT WHISKY
LIQUEUR

NOTABLE WEEKENDS!

ESCAPE FOR A WEEKEND WITH MOZART, HAYDN, CHOPIN OR RACHMANINOFF

The definition of a perfect weekend — the charm and ambiance of a historic Heritage Hotel and the classical music of the masters, flawlessly performed. Come and celebrate the 35th Anniversary Season of *Music at Leisure* at a Heritage Hotel. Imagine sitting in The Chaucer Hotel overlooking the ancient walls of Canterbury, hearing Schubert's *Death and the Maiden* performed by The Alberni String Quartet. Or relaxing at Leeming House, with its wooded gardens and scenic lake, awash in Beethoven's *Moonlight Sonata*, brilliantly performed by pianist Noriko Ogawa. ☎ Each of our twelve weekends offers a unique musical experience on Friday and Saturday evenings, in a house party atmosphere, with fine dining, wonderful service, and the historic sights of Britain just outside the door. ☎

A notable experience indeed!

To make a reservation or for more information, call 034 554 3555

Heritage Hotels – Ross-on-Wye
The Royal

Palace Pound, Ross-on-Wye, HR9 5HZ See map page 7 Tel (0)870 400 8124 Fax: (0)198 976 8058
Regional General Manager: James Lever E-mail:HeritageHotels_Ross_on_Wye@forte-hotels.com

The Royal has a spectacular outlook across Horseshoe Bend on the River Wye. Queen Victoria enjoyed it so much at the time of her visit that she stayed to afternoon tea. Originally built on the site of the old Bishop's Palace, it has had sympathetic modernisation over the years, but remains proud of its many historical associations. Charles Dickens was a visitor in 1867, hence the Dickens Lounge and the bedrooms named after characters in his books.

Attractions: Rock cliffs, fine walking. The Forest of Dean, the "Queen of Forests" (wildlife, rare birds, even the occasional wild boar). Malvern Hills, Brecon Beacons. 12th-century ruins of Goodrich Castle. Monmouth Castle. (Horse) Racing at Chepstow. Hay-on-Wye (second-hand book capital of the world). Facilities for swimming, squash, tennis, potholing and riding. Birds of Prey Centre.

How to get there
14 miles from Hereford and 17 from Gloucester, the Royal is located near the hamlet of Wilton. 1 mile off the M50 you cross Wilton Bridge and then turn on to the slip road that leads to the hotel.

Facilities: 40 bedrooms, 1 half-tester, hairdryer, trouser press, restaurant, bar, lounge, open fires in winter, free car park.
Family: Baby listening.

Special Break rates
April–October
Mid-week/Weekend
£185
November–March
Mid-week/Weekend
£180
Prices are per person for two nights with all activities mentioned included.
(Excludes 22–28 August, 23–27 December and 30 December–2 January 2000)

Special Break
Relax and experience the warmth of traditional hospitality at the Royal. As an old coaching inn, steeped in history with past guests such as Queen Victoria and Charles Dickens, this hotel provides guests with a warm welcome, cosy atmosphere and spectacular food.

Arrive from 2pm onwards and enjoy a Herefordshire cream tea in the Dickens Lounge or in the charming gardens overlooking the River Wye's Horseshoe Bend.

A superb 3-course evening meal with coffee will be served in the Shires Restaurant with a welcome sherry.

Start your day by indulging in a hearty breakfast before leaving for Monmouth Golf Club in the Wye Valley for 18 holes of superb golf. Alternatively, non-golfers shouldn't miss the opportunity to visit the Map of Mundi within the famous Hereford Cathedral, and on the way back try a River Cruise at Symonds Yat East.

Return to the Hotel to freshen up before a well-earned 3-course dinner and half a bottle of house wine per person. Relax with coffee in the Dickens Lounge and try out the hotel's chess board.

After a leisurely breakfast why not stroll along the River Wye or visit the interesting shops in the town; all before a 3-course Sunday lunch prior to your journey home.

What's included in your break:
- 2 nights' dinner, bed and breakfast
- Herefordshire cream tea
- 3-course evening meal with coffee, a half-bottle of house wine per person and a welcome sherry (day 1)
- green fee to Monmouth Golf Club (18 holes) or visit the Hereford Cathedral and a river cruise at Symonds Yat East
- 3-course lunch (day 3)

Ross-on-Wye

DRIVING ROUTE

The B4234 south out of Ross-on-Wye passes Goodrich Castle, then joins the B4229 to the A40 down to Monmouth. From here, take the A466 south to Tintern Abbey. Minor roads off the B4228 lead in to the Forest of Dean. The A4136 leads out of the forest and onto the B4216 to Ledbury. The A449 leads back to Ross-on-Wye.

The medieval Goodrich Castle.

❶ Goodrich Castle

Goodrich was largely destroyed during the English Civil War, but prior to that its fortifications had been an important stronghold since the 12th century. The 14th-century banqueting hall can still be seen.

❷ Monmouth Castle

Set on the Welsh border, this 11th-century castle is now little more than a ruin, but its hill has commanding views over the region. The town of Monmouth is also notable as the birthplace of King Henry V.

❸ Tintern Abbey

This 12th-century Cistercian abbey includes a Gothic-style church and remnants of the former monks' quarters illustrating the harshness of monastic life. The abbey rose to particular fame when William Wordsworth composed his famous poem on the subject.

❺ Ledbury

Ledbury is one of the finest preserved Tudor towns in the country and numerous buildings from this era line its streets, including the Market Hall, which is still used for its original purpose at weekends.

❹ Forest of Dean

Most famous for its ancient and majestic oak trees, the forest is perennially popular with ramblers and picnickers. It was also a centre of iron ore mining but this ecologically destructive practice was stopped in the 17th century.

Bluebells carpet the floor of many parts of the Forest of Dean.

Heritage Hotels – St Andrews
Rusacks

Plimour Links, St Andrews, Fife KY16 9JQ See map page 13 Tel: (0)870 400 8128 Fax: (0)133 447 7896
Regional General Manager: Joe Longmuir E-mail: HeritageHotels_StAndrews.Rusacks@forte-hotels.com

Guests who have stayed at Rusacks include golfing and rock and roll legends. Originally opened in 1887, it has been stylishly remodelled on a golfing theme to take advantage of its prestigious location and eye-catching views over the 18th green of the Old Course. The Old Course Bar and Restaurant, which has a dramatic view of the famous course, specialises in seafood and game dishes.

How to get there
Rusacks Hotel sits adjacent to the coastal A91, with junction 8 of the M90 26 miles away.

Facilities: 44 bedrooms, 4 suites, many rooms overlooking the golf course and St Andrews Bay, 24-hour room service, hairdryer, trouser press, satellite TV, golf club, bar, log fires in winter, free car park. Sauna and solarium.
Family: baby listening.

Special Break rates
£60 per person supplement to the Leisure Break Rate Validity dates: until 31–March 2000
(Excludes 23–29 April, 22–26 June, 12–21 July, 5–13 October, 18–19 October, 23–27 December 1999, 30 December–2 January 2000)

Special Break
Turn your Forte Leisure Break into the perfect golfer's indulgence: take tips from one of St Andrew's PGA Professionals with a golf lesson captured on video for posterity. Back in the comfort of your home, what better way to remember your relaxing break than re-living your lesson accompanied by a dram of whisky from your new engraved decanter and glasses. This special gift from the hotel depicts St Andrews and the Swilken Bridge, the ideal souvenir of a trip to the Home of Golf.

Attractions: An in-house gold club, including changing rooms, a sauna solarium, pro-shop and bar. Themed rooms around the history of golf in St Andrews. Light meals served all day. Resident golf manager.

St Andrews

DRIVING ROUTE

Take the A91, turning left at Kincaple. Drive south, passing through Denhead and turn east onto the B940 to Lochty. Then take the right hand fork, crossing over the B9171. Turn left onto the A917 to Anstruther, then travel northeast on the A917 to Crail. The Scottish Bunker is signposted off the B940.

➊ St Andrews

The centre of life in St Andrews is its university, the oldest in Scotland, and tours of the 15th-century buildings are possible. The cathedral is also an important historic sight. It dates from the 12th century but was fell into ruin during the Reformation.

➋ Royal and Ancient Golf Club

St Andrews is a mecca for golfers around the world, and the Royal and Ancient dates from the 1750s. The British Open is held at the Old Course, where there is also a museum of golfing greats.

The harbour at the fishing village of Crail.

➍ Crail

One of the most attractive of the fishing villages along this coast also benefits from a beach and a golf course. A taste of the seafood that gives the village its livelihood is recommended in one of the restaurants.

Golfers at the Royal and Ancient Golf Club, in St Andrews.

➌ Anstruther

The main industry of this small town is fishing, and a museum dedicated to the industry makes a fascinating visit. An old fisherman's cottage and a boatyard are part of the display.

➎ Scottish Bunker

A simple farmhouse is the "undercover" entrance of this bunker, which was set up during the Cold War for government use in case of nuclear attack. In 1994 it was opened to the public as a museum, dedicated to the 1950s era of nuclear obsession.

Heritage Hotels – Salisbury

The White Hart

St John Street, Salisbury, Wiltshire SP1 2SD See map page 4 Tel: (0)870 400 8125 Fax: (0)172 241 2761
Regional General Manager: Michael Grange E-mail: HeritageHotels_Salisbury.White_Hart@forte-hotels.com

A Georgian landmark with sweeping facade and pillared portico, the architecture of the White Hart has undergone some sympathetic 20th-century restoration. Try the luxury of the St Catherine suite with its balcony over the portico, one of the three rooms with glorious four-posters. In winter, huge log fires burn in open fireplaces, and in summer months the courtyard is a tapestry of colour with flower displays. Salisbury is ringed by prehistoric forts and mystic stone circles, the most famous one being Stonehenge.

How to get there
Follow the ring road to its southernmost point and then turn into Exeter Street, towards the city centre. The hotel is on the right-hand side.

Facilities: 68 bedrooms, 3 four-posters, restaurant, lounge and bar, open fires in winter, free car park.
Family: baby listening, baby-sitting on request.

Attractions: Salisbury Cathedral with its 404-ft spire. Yarbury Castle. Clearbury Ring. Figsbury Ring. Old Roman villa at Rockbourne. Wilton House designed by Inigo Jones. Antiques Fair in March. St George's Festival in April. Salisbury Festival of Music in May. South England Flower Show in June. Local leisure facilities: swimming, squash, tennis, snooker, sauna, horse-riding and golf.

A White Hart Connoisseur Break rates
2-night programme
£175 per person
(April–October), £160
(November–March)
Valid to March 2000
(Excludes 23–27 December
and 30 December–2 January
2000)

A White Hart Connoisseur Break
Arriving on Friday night to a warm welcome in your comfortable bedroom, with every amenity for gracious living. In the bedroom you will find a welcome gift of chilled champagne, chocolates and a complimentary guidebook to the city.

Savour a candlelit dinner in the restaurant from the full à la carte menu followed by a complimentary liqueur or cognac with your coffee in the delightful lounge or courtyard.

After a relaxing night's sleep, explore the city on the guided walk from the Guild Hall and then in the afternoon take in the magnificent cathedral with the tallest spire in Britain. Return to the hotel for a traditional cream tea.

On Saturday evening enjoy another fine dinner in the restaurant and after a comfortable night,

depart after breakfast on Sunday via Winchester and the Wessex Hotel to enjoy a traditional Sunday lunch and tour this fascinating city.

What's included in your break:
• 2 nights' dinner, bed and breakfast
• a welcome gift of champagne and chocolates
• a guidebook to the city of Salisbury
• 3-course dinner from the full à la carte menu (wine not included)
• complimentary liqueur or cognac with your coffee
• full English breakfast both days
• full traditional tea (Saturday)
• traditional Sunday lunch at the Wessex Heritage Hotel (Winchester)

Salisbury

Driving Route

Drive west out of Salisbury to Wilton then north to the A303, where Stonehenge is visible from the road. From here take the A303, turning north on the B3092 to Stourhead. Follow the B3092 south again, joining the B3081 at Gillingham and continue southest to Shaftesbury.

① Salisbury Cathedral

This 13th-century cathedral has the tallest spire in England, reaching 404 feet, and can be seen from miles around. The interior is notable for its natural light, and its library, which contains an original copy of the Magna Carta.

Stained glass window at Salisbury Cathedral.

② Wilton House

This Elizabethan house was designed by the great architect Inigo Jones and is one of the finest stately homes in England. It is worth a visit for its art collection, and for the illustrations of scenes from Arcadia, written by the 16th-century poet Sir Philip Sidney while he was living at Wilton.

③ Stonehenge

One of Britain's most famous and precious sites, and a UNESCO World Heritage Site, this prehistoric stone circle still baffles historians. Dating as far back as 3000BC, it is also not known how these massive stones were transported here. But these mysteries all add to the attraction.

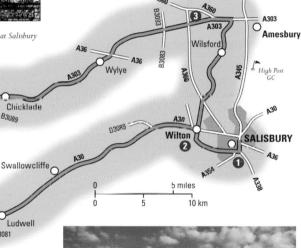

④ Stourhead

The main attraction of this stately home is its beautiful, landscaped gardens, reminiscent of Renaissance Italy. The owner commissioned the design in the 1750s, filling the grounds with lakes, bridges and statues, among other features.

⑤ Shaftesbury

The most familiar image of Shaftesbury is Gold Hill. Its steep incline, cobbled street and quaint houses have made it a feature of advertising campaigns and innumerable photographs.

The stone circle at Stonehenge has been a site of pagan rituals for thousands of years. Even today, the summer solstice is celebrated in the area.

Heritage Hotels – Sherborne
The Sherborne

Horsecastles Lane, Sherborne, Dorset DT9 6BB See map page 3 Tel: (0)870 400 8127 Fax: (0)193 581 3191
Regional General Manager: Brian Shanahan E-mail: HeritageHotels_Sherborne.Sherborne@forte-hotels.com

The Sherborne Hotel stands in four acres of grounds, with a garden terrace where pupils from the famous public school at Sherborne can be over-indulged on cream teas when their parents come to visit. The Castles Restaurant – the name paying tribute to the two ancient castles in the town – offers a traditional English menu. Small delightful Dorset villages abound.

How to get there
The Sherborne Hotel is on the junction of the A30 and the A352.

Facilities: 59 bedrooms, all with hairdryer, trouser press and TV, 11 family rooms, restaurant, bar, lounge with satellite TV, croquet lawn, putting green (seasonal), free car park.
Family: baby listening, baby-sitting (by prior arrangement).

Attractions: Sherborne's historic associations. Golf. Walking. Yeovil.

Special Break rates
A 3-night break
May–October 1999
£155 per person
November 1999–March 2000
£135 per person
(Excludes 23–26 December and 30 December–2 January 2000)

Special Break
Be welcomed with champagne and chocolates in your room. Enjoy dinner in the Castles Restaurant each night with complimentary house wine. On Saturday enjoy a complimentary visit to the famous Haynes Motor Museum, a collection of over 250 classic to exotic cars. On Sunday, take a leisurely drive to the historic city of Exeter and enjoy a traditional Sunday lunch at the Southgate Hotel, again included in the break. Return to Sherborne at leisure for dinner and overnight stay.

What's included in your break:
- champagne and chocolates in your room on arrival
- 3 nights' accommodation
- 3-course menu dinner every night (a bottle of house wine per couple included every night)
- ticket to the Haynes Motor Museum
- Sunday lunch at the Southgate Hotel in Exeter

Sherborne

DRIVING ROUTE

Take the A352 south out of Sherborne and the Cerne Abbas giant will be seen on your left about seven miles further on. Contine along this road to reach Dorchester, and Maiden Castle, on the outskirts of the town. The A354 leads south to the coast and Weymouth, then follow the B3157 west towards Bridport, joining the A35 to reach Lyme Regis.

❶ Cerne Abbas

The main feature of this Dorset town is the "giant" carved into the chalk-based hill. Generally considered to be an ancient fertility symbol, many childless couples come here in the hope of conceiving after their visit.

Boats moored at the dock in the seaside town of Weymouth.

❹ Weymouth

King George III popularised Weymouth when he holidayed here in the 18th century, and as a result this quiet seaside town, still a regular holiday destination for many, is littered with elegant Georgian architecture.

❺ Lyme Regis

One of the prettiest seaside towns on the English coast, Lyme Regis is best known for it limestone and clay foundations, which allowed fossils of, among other things, a dinosaur skeleton, to be uncovered here in 1811. The town again achieved international fame in the 1980s when it was used as the location for the film *The French Lieutenant's Woman.*

❷ Dorchester

The heart of "Hardy Country", Dorchester was named as Casterbridge in the novels of Thomas Hardy, who was born near here and used the area as the setting for all his books. The town's museum re-creates Hardy's study and includes an exhibition on his work.

❸ Maiden Castle

Now little more than a mound, the attraction of Maiden Castle lies in its history as a Stone Age settlement. The area thrived until the arrival of the Romans and archaeological digs have uncovered priceless prehistoric artefacts, now on display in Dorchester's museum.

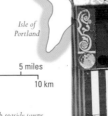

Isle of Portland

```
0            5 miles
|---+---+---|
0      5      10 km
```

Traditional English seaside towns have many quaint attractions, such as piers, fish-and-chip shops and, of course, Punch and Judy shows

Punch and Judy Shows

Heritage Hotels – Staines
The Thames Lodge

Thames Street, Staines, Middx TW18 4SE See map page 4 Tel: (0)870 400 8121 Fax: (0)178 445 4858
Regional General Manager: Ben Godon E-mail: HeritageHotels_Staines.Thames_Loche@forte-hotels.com

A rambling, mainly 19th-century building with a modern extension sitting right on the banks of the river, the hotel still has its own moorings, a tradition dating back to the days when it was known as the Packhorse and was used as a stopping spot for barges being hauled up the river by horses. Visitors enjoy the sights of the river from the lounge and the Brasserie Restaurant and those who have plumped for a bedroom on the top floor have an almost panoramic view, which makes it easy to forget that this hotel is only 19 miles from central London.

Attractions: Thames Lodge Conference Centre (converted cottages with direct access to the hotel's riverside terrace). Racing at Royal Ascot. Kempton Park and Sandown racecourses. Kew. Windsor Castle. Hampton Court. Signing of the Magna Carta at Runnymede. Runnymede Country Show mid-August. Windsor Castle. Old Father Thames. Legoland and Thorpe Park.

How to get there
Leave the M25 at junction 13 and join the A30 to London. At Crooked Billet roundabout, follow signs for Staines town centre. On one-way system in Staines, stay in right-hand lane until T-junction, hotel is directly in front of you. Car park is on the left

Facilities: 79 bedrooms, hairdryer, trouser press, brasserie and terrace overlooking the Thames, bar, lounge, function suites.

Special Break rates
Validity dates: 1 June 1999 – 31 March 2000
£125 per person (based on two people sharing)
Single supplement £10 per person per night
(Excludes 23–26 December and 30 December–2 January

Special Break
Day 1 – Arrive at your leisure, check in to one of the recently refurbished rooms, and enjoy dinner in the Brasserie Restaurant overlooking the River Thames.

Day 2 – After breakfast, you are invited to visit Hampton Court with the hotel's compliments. This is England's finest royal palace, with over 500 years of history, and is situated on the banks of the River Thames. Follow in the footsteps of some of the greatest kings and queens through the magnificent state apartments, Great Hall and Chapel Royal.

In the afternoon, a visit to Windsor Castle is recommended,

Return to the hotel to relax with an aperitif in the lounge and reflect over dinner on the wonders of the day.

Day 3 – After a hearty English breakfast, checking out of the hotel, and before you leave for home, we recommend either a walk along the River Thames at Eaton, or a visit to the beautiful Saville Gardens.

What's included in your break:
- 2 nights' dinner, bed and breakfast
- ticket to Hampton Court (opens every day except 24th–26th December. Mid-March to mid-October 9.30am to 6pm. Last admission 45 minutes before closing)
- 3-course table d'hôte dinner menu (coffee included)

Staines

*Late afternoon at
Virginia Water,
in the snow.*

DRIVING ROUTE

Runnymede can be found off the A308 en route to
Windsor. Then take the A328 and the A30 through
Egham to see Royal Holloway College. Virginia Water
is on the B389, which passes under the M25 and turns
into the B388 and the location of Thorpe Park, off the
A320. From here take the B375 and A244 to Sunbury
and turn east onto the A308 to reach Kempton Park.

❶ Runnymede

On 15 June 1215, King John signed the *Magna Carta*
at Runnymede, a document that not only prevented
civil war in his reign, but laid down the foundations
of a justice system that exists today throughout the
civilised world. A memorial marks the
site of this historic event.

❷ Royal Holloway College

Modelled on a French
chateau, the grand
building, which now
houses part
of the
University of
London, was
constructed
in the 1880s for
Thomas Holloway as a
women's college.
Turrets and gables help
to conjure up the
intended castle
imagery. Inside the
main college building is
a fine collection of
Victorian art.

❸ Virginia Water

This pretty Surrey village was also subject to Thomas
Holloway's vision, as the site for his Holloway
Sanatorium. Rumour has it that there is a secret
underground passage between the college and the
sanatorium, but this has never been proved.

*The Thunder River Ride is the
most popular attraction at Thorpe
Park.*

❹ Thorpe Park

A theme park whose
emphasis is largely
placed on water, such
as Thunder River white
water ride. It is
particularly popular
with children, who
enjoy the soaking that is
the result of almost
every ride.

❺ Kempton Racecourse

Often dubbed
"London's racecourse",
Kempton Park is the
nearest racing circuit to
the capital, making it a
popular day-trip for
avid race-goers. A
statue of the award-
winning horse Desert
Orchid overlooks the
Parade ground.

The Alveston Manor

Clopton Bridge, Stratford-upon-Avon, CV37 7HP See map page 4 Tel: (0)870 400 8181 Fax: (0)178 941 4095
Regional General Manager: Sean Sullivan E-mail: HeritageHotels_Stratford_upon_Avon.Alveston_Manor@forte-hotels.com

This is one of the finest bases from which to explore Stratford and surrounding areas. Visitors here (among them Harrison Ford and Bob Dylan – pursuing the legends and life of the world's greatest writer) discover that the first performance of *A Midsummer's Night Dream* was given under the cedar tree that stands in the hotel's grounds. Leaded windows and an oak-panelled bar are mellow features of this hotel, as is the silver carving trolley in the award-winning Manor Grill.

Attractions: Tudor panelling and Elizabethan staircase. (OCCASIONAL) Summertime presentations of A Midsummer's Night Dream beneath the ancient cedar tree. A vaulted cellar leads to an underground passage once used by monks from Worcester. Nearby Warwick Castle. Gateway to the Cotswolds.

Tennis, golf.

How to get there
Leave the M40 at junction 15, taking the A46 and the A439 towards Stratford. Join the one-way system, and keeping left towards Banbury and Oxford you'll find The Alveston Manor just over the bridge at the junction of the A422 and the A3400.

Facilities: 114 bedrooms, 6 suites, room service, hairdryer, trouser press, satellite TV, Manor Grill (AA Rosette), terrace/bar, free car park.
Family: Baby-listening.

Shakespeare's Stratford at the Alveston Manor rates
The rate for this special theatre weekend is £200 per person for two nights, based on two people sharing a standard twin or double room. Supplements apply for upgrade to suites and executive accommodation. Weekends only from June 1999–end March 2000, plus any 2 nights between 21 July and 30 August 1999. (Excludes 23–26 December and 30 December–2 January 2000) Available any weekend, subject to availability.

Shakespeare's Stratford at the Alveston Manor
The home of the Bard offers you a superb two-night theatre break at the Alveston Manor, where history is blended with modernity, creating a relaxing and comfortable location in the heart of England. Set on the south side of the River Avon, a five-minute walk across the ancient bridge will take you to interesting shops, the world-renowned theatre and the famous Shakespeare properties. The river bank is alive with narrow boats and wild fowl, the water meadows ideal for a leisurely walk on a beautiful evening, whatever the season. On arrival on Friday, you will find a bottle of champagne in your room, with flowers, chocolates and bathrobes. Dinner on your first night will be in the Manor Grill, with a pre-dinner Pimm's awaiting you in the cocktail bar. After breakfast on Saturday, tickets for the superb Guide Friday tour of Stratford in an open-topped bus will be available. While you are out and about, lunch in Othello's Bistro in the centre of town (included in your package), will fortify you for the afternoon's sightseeing. Before departing for the

theatre, your starter and main course will be served in the Manor Grill, with post-theatre dessert and liqueur at the hotel on your return. The Royal Shakespeare Theatre offers critically acclaimed productions throughout the year and no visit to Stratford-upon-Avon would be complete without this experience. After breakfast, before you depart, a copy of last night's play will be presented to you as a memento of your stay.

What's included in your break:
- 2 nights' dinner, bed and breakfast
- champagne, chocolates and flowers on arrival
- pre-dinner glass of Pimm's on Friday night
- tickets for Guide Friday tour of Stratford-upon-Avon on Saturday
- lunch in Othello's Bistro on Saturday
- two tickets for Saturday evening performance at the Royal Shakespeare Theatre
- one copy per couple of the play enjoyed
- complimentary copy of the performance programme

Stratford-upon-Avon

DRIVING ROUTE

The A3400 leads on to the A429 and southwest to Moreton-in-Marsh. Take the B4035 to Chipping Campden, then the B4081 and A44 to reach Broadway. Continue on toward Evesham and go north along the A46 to Ragley Hall. The A46 leads back to Stratford, and Charlecote Park is northeast of the town, off the B4086.

The mansion at Charlecote Park.

❶ Moreton-in-Marsh

The main attraction of this Cotswolds town is the Batsford Arboretum, a landscaped garden planted with, among other species, Japanese and Chinese trees.

❷ Chipping Campden

An authentic medieval town, and one of the most attractive in the area, Chipping Campden thrived on the wool industry. Today it buzzes again during the Cotswolds Games, a festival of bizarre but amusing country games.

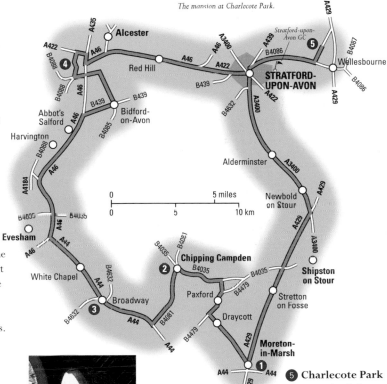

❸ Broadway

Perhaps the most famous, and certainly the most visited of all Cotswolds towns, Broadway is named after its long main street, now littered with souvenir shops. The original stone architecture of the houses is lovingly preserved.

Cobbled walkway at Chipping Campden.

❹ Ragley Hall

Ragley Hall was designed in 1680 by Robert Hooke, in the Palladian style, emulating the Venetian architect Andrea Palladio. Inside is a priceless collection of furniture and art.

❺ Charlecote Park

The Lucy family have occupied this site since 1247, and the park's mansion includes many memorials to past ancestors. The gardens, which include a croquet lawn accessible for public use, are still inhabited by roaming deer.

Heritage Hotels – Stratford-upon-Avon
The Shakespeare

Chapel Street, Stratford-upon-Avon, CV37 6ER See map page 4 Tel: (0)870 400 8183 Fax: (0)178 941 5411
Regional General Manager: Sean Sullivan E-mail: HeritageHotels_Stratford_upon_Avon.Shakespeare@forte-hotels.com

The old stone floor remains in the reception area of this black and white Tudor-fronted hotel. Prince Charles has been here, as has Margaret Thatcher. In fact, the hotel's guest list has included many renowned names, particularly politicians, foreign diplomats and dedicated scholars pursuing the life and works of Shakespeare (including Elizabeth Taylor while engaged in the *Taming of the Shrew*, filmed with Richard Burton). Fittingly, each guest room bears the title of one of his plays. The Othello Restaurant has a traditional menu and an award-winning chef.

How to get there
Leave the M40 at junction 15, taking the A46 and the A 439 towards Stratford. Join the one-way system, take Bridge Street to the roundabout and then left into the High Street, which leads into Chapel Street.

Facilites: 70 bedrooms, 3 four-posters, 1 suite, hairdryer, trouser press, David Garrick Restaurant (AA Rosette), bistro, cocktail bar, lounge, open fire in winter, free parking (limited).
Family: Baby listening, baby-sitting.

Attractions: Music at Leisure and Break for Murder weekends. Stratford-upon-Avon Theatre. Cox's Yard, an interactive centre. Charlecoat Park (where legend has it Shakespeare was caught poaching by the owner). Warwick Castle (the finest medieval castle in England). The Cotswolds.

Stratford-upon-Avon

WALKING ROUTE:

The majority of these sights are all within easy walking distance. From Shakespeare's Birthplace, walk down Guild Street to Waterside and the site of the Royal Shakespeare Theatre. Continuing west along Southern Lane, Hall's Croft is on your right along Old Town, and the Holy Trinity Church on your left along Trinity Street. Anne Hathaway's cottage is about one mile out of the town centre, but a tourist bus runs to the area regularly.

❶ Shakespeare's Birthplace

Although it has never actually been proved that the great playwright was born here, these two-houses-in-one are treated as genuine. The interior is furnished as a 16th-century home, emulating how Shakespeare may have lived, as well as displaying many items that belonged to him.

❷ Royal Shakespeare Theatre

As its name suggest, the programme of performances here centres almost entirely on the many plays of Shakespeare. Backstage tours of the costumes and props departments are available.

❹ Hall's Croft

Shakespeare's daughter Susanna married the doctor John Hall and lived with him in this house. Today it houses an often unnerving museum dedicated to Elizabethan medicine.

❸ Holy Trinity Church

In a town obsessed with its past resident, the main claim to fame of this church is the burial tomb of Shakespeare himself. But moving away from the crowds, it is possible to appreciate the fine Gothic structure, which predates its well-known occupant.

The Royal Shakespeare Theatre, at night.

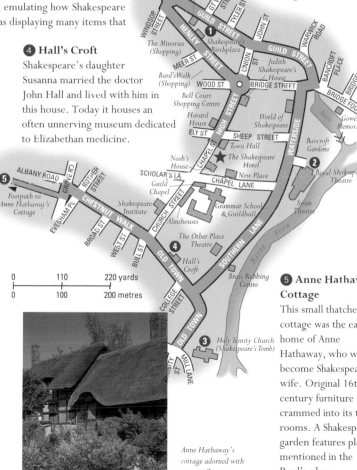

Anne Hathaway's cottage adorned with summer flowers.

❺ Anne Hathaway's Cottage

This small thatched cottage was the early home of Anne Hathaway, who would become Shakespeare's wife. Original 16th-century furniture is crammed into its tiny rooms. A Shakespeare garden features plants mentioned in the Bard's plays.

The Great British Heritage Pass 1999

BRITAIN

Dramatic castles, beautiful stately homes and gardens and medieval manor houses are yours to discover with the Great British Heritage Pass – our invitation to the independent traveller to visit almost 600 of Britain's finest historic properties free of charge.*

The handy pass gives you a rare opportunity to explore a wide variety of properties as described in your free gazetteer and located in whichever part of the country you are planning to travel. The National Trust, English Heritage, other heritage organisations and many privately-owned properties are all part of the pass.

How long is the pass valid and how much does it cost?

There are three types of passes available; a **7-day pass** *(£30)*, a **15-day pass** *(£42)* and a **1-month pass** *(£56 or local currency equivalent).*

For your free brochure and order form please call your local BTA office.

* The Tower of London is half-price, all other properties give free entry with the pass.

EOA

BRITISH TOURIST AUTHORITY

Heritage Hotels – Stratford-upon-Avon
The Swan's Nest

Bridgefoot, Stratford-upon-Avon, CV37 7LT See map page 4 Tel: (0)870 400 8182 Fax: (0)178 941 4547
Regional General Manager: Sean Sullivan E-mail: HeritageHotel_Stratford_upon_Avon.Swans_Nest@forte-hotels.com

This hotel dates from the late 17th century and is one of the earliest brick houses built in the Stratford area. With its own river frontage, it is perfectly situated for an afternoon boating trip, or a leisurely stroll along the banks of the Avon before heading for the theatre, just a five-minute walk away. There is the River Bar, the informal Cygnet Restaurant with pre-theatre dinners and, after an unusually long performance, 24-hour room service.

How to get there
Leave the M40 at junction 15, taking the A46 for 2 miles. First island turn left onto A439 towards Stratford. Follow one-way system, turn left (A3400), over the bridge, the Swan's Nest is on the right.

Facilities: 68 bedrooms, restaurant, bar, lounge, free parking.
Family: baby listening

Attractions: Shakespeare's Stratford. Gateway to the Cotswolds. Warwick Castle. Charlecote Park (where rumour has it that Shakespeare was once caught poaching by the owner).

Stratford-upon-Avon

DRIVING ROUTE

Take the A3400 then the A4189; the A435 leads to the Birmingham suburb of Bournville. From here take the A4040 to the A45, and at Stonebridge journey south along the A452 to Kenilworth. Warwick lies to the south on the A46, and Leamington Spa is northeast of here. Take the A425 to Daventry; Althorp is five miles east of here on the A428.

Jephson Gardens at Leamington Spa.

④ Leamington Spa

Like many of England's spa towns, Leamington Spa rose to prominence in the 18th century. The Royal Pump Room is still used for its original purpose, as a place to take the medicinal waters and various spa treatments.

① Bournville

The Cadbury family set up their famous chocolate-making factory in this suburb of Birmingham, and today a museum takes visitors through the process of production as well as offering free tastings at the end of the tour. Chocolate bars may be purchased at wholesale prices in the shop.

Re-creation of a battle scene at Kenilworth Castle.

② Kenilworth Castle

Home to John of Gaunt and Henry IV, this 12th-century castle became the home of the popular Earl of Leicester in the 16th century. The Civil War left it in ruins, but it remains an impressive nod to history.

③ Warwick Castle

One of the most popular but macabre features of this vast 14th-century castle is a tour of the dungeon, where unfortunate prisoners were left to rot in isolation. Much of the castle is littered with "authentic" waxwork figures of royalty, courtesy of the castle's new owners, Madame Tussauds.

⑤ Althorp

This 16th-century mansion may have passed unnoticed among England's many stately homes, had it not been the childhood home of Lady Diana Spencer, later Princess of Wales. She is buried on a small island in a lake, which is not accessible to tourists. Her brother, Earl Spencer, has built a museum in her memory, which is open each summer.

Heritage Hotels ~ Ullswater

Leeming House

Watermillock, Ullswater, Nr Penrith, Cumbria CA11 0JJ See map page 10 Tel:(0)870 400 8131 Fax:(0)176 848 6443
Regional General Manager: Colin Campbell E-mail: HeritageHotels.Leeming_House@forte-hotels.com

O nce the private residence of the local Bolton family, this 200-year-old estate is surrounded by 20 acres of lush gardens in the heart of the glorious Lake District countryside. The Regency Restaurant, with its modern and classic menu that specialises in local produce, was chosen as the 1999 Lake District Restaurant of the Year.

How to get there
Leave the M6 and then follow the A66 and the A592 to Ullswater and Windermere. Soon you will reach Watermillock by Ullswater. The hotel is about 2 miles further on.

Facilities: 39 bedrooms, 1 mini suite, 24-hour room service, hairdryer, trouser press, satellite TV, the Regency Restaurant (smart dress), the Conservatory, cocktail bar, private dining, drawing room, library and sitting room, open log fires in winter, garden, croquet lawn, private fishing, helipad, free car park.
Family: baby listening, baby-sitting.

Lakeland Discovered rates
Price per person for two nights
May–October 1999
Fri/Sat–£330
Sun/Thur–£280
November 1999–April 2000
Fri/Sat–£280
Sun/Thur–£260
Upgrade to rooms with private balcony and overlooking gardens towards the lake £15 supplement per person per night
(Excludes 23–26 December and 30 December–2 January 2000)

Attractions: The famous "Tree Trail", a half-mile of variegated woodland with trees from all over the world (guests are supplied with descriptive map). Ideal spot for walking, sailing, horse-riding, trekking, golfing and motorised biking (quadbiking) into the hills. Ornithologists will appreciate the local Bird of Prey Centre.

Lakeland Discovered
The tranquil and relaxing charms of Lake Ullswater await on a two-night break at this special country house hotel, a world away from the commercial pressures of everyday life and yet only seven miles from the M6 motorway.

The hotel is set in its own 20 acres of gardens, leading to the famous water where Wordsworth discovered his daffodils, and the endangered red squirrel can be frequently spotted.

Your room on arrival will have champagne, flowers, chocolates and bathrobes.

Dinner will be a relaxing affair with award-winning cuisine provided by our chef Adam Marks, followed by coffee and petits fours in one of lounges.

Following breakfast, transportation to Windermere is arranged, where you will join some fellow explorers on a journey over the high and twisting passes of the Western Fells. With lots of stops throughout the day you will enjoy visits to locations such as Hardknott Roman Forte, Eskdale, Wasdale and Muncaster Castle Gardens and Owl Sanctuary. There is also a train ride on the famous miniature railway at Eskdale.

A gourmet dinner, prepared specially, with wine, awaits your return, then perhaps a stroll around the gardens to close the day.

Breakfast prior to departure with a last chance to explore before your journey home.

What's included in your break:
• 2 nights' dinner, bed and breakfast
• champagne, chocolates and flowers
• full-day excursion in west Cumbria
• ride on Ravensglass & Eskdale steam railway
• admission to Muncaster Castle Gardens and Owl Sanctuary
• 1 bottle house wine per couple on second night

116

Ullswater

DRIVING ROUTE

Ullswater is on the A592 and Gowbarrow Park is north of Glenridding on the same road. A footpath from Glenridding leads to the peak of Helvellyn. Proceed north back along the A592 to Penrith, then take either the M6 or A6 to Carlisle.

❶ Ullswater

This meandering lake is one of the most scenic in the region. The Ullswater Steamer crosses the lake and is a popular means of transport for both tourists and locals.

❷ Gowbarrow Park

The most famous sight in this lakeside park can be seen in the spring, when the land bursts into bloom in a carpet of daffodils. Wordsworth dedicated his most famous poem to the flower.

❸ Helvellyn

This 3000-ft mountain is one of the more popular hikes in the Lake District. The climb is steep and rocky, but the views across the region from the summit make the effort worthwhile.

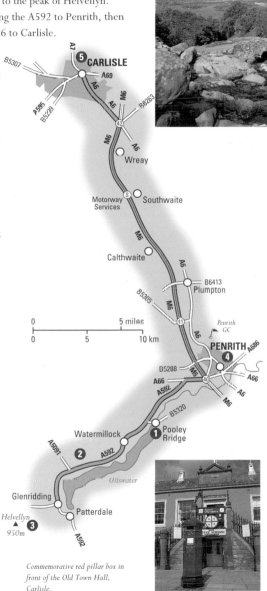

If you enjoy hiking, the Lake District is an ideal place to visit. Here you can enjoy exhilarating trails and spectacular scenery.

Commemorative red pillar box in front of the Old Town Hall, Carlisle.

❹ Penrith

Penrith Castle is now little more than a ruin, but its existence illustrates the importance of this town in the 14th century, when it was constantly under threat from its northern neighbours.

❺ Carlisle

Elizabeth I imprisoned Mary, Queen of Scots in Carlisle Castle in the 16th century. The town has traditionally been a warring point between England and Scotland. Details of this period, and its earlier Roman history, are explained in the town's museum. In the centre of town is a beautiful 18th-century Old Town Hall.

Heritage Hotels – Winchester
The Wessex

Paternoster Row, Winchester, Hants SO23 9LQ See map page 4 Tel: (0)870 400 8126 Fax: (0)196 284 1503
Regional General Manager: Michael Grange E-mail: HeritageHotels_Winchester.Wessex@forte-hotels.com

The Wessex overlooks Winchester's magnificent 900-year-old cathedral, where the famous remains laid to rest include St Swithin, Jane Austen and many of the ancient kings of England. Its central location is ideally suited for strolling and soaking up the historic atmosphere of this city. Hardy, Trollope and Keats all spent time in Winchester and included the city in their writings. The William Walker Restaurant serves a speciality fish menu, and the cream teas are a high spot of the afternoons.

How to get there
Take the M3 and leave at junction 9. Turn left into the one-way system, stay in the left-hand lane and then right at the next roundabout into Broadway. Turn left into Colebrook Street and the Wessex is on your right.

Facilities: 91 bedrooms, 3 suites, 24-hour room service, hairdryer, satellite TV, restaurant, lounge bar, free car parking (for residents).
Family: Baby-sitting.

Attractions: Winchester Cathedral, the Cathedral Close and Dean Garnier's Garden; the Great Hall and King Arthur's Round Table; the remains of Hyde Abbey where King Alfred is buried; Water Meadows, inspiration for Keat's poem "Ode to Autumn"; Winchester College; antiques in Jewry Street; antiquarian bookshops; good fishing.

A King Alfred's Connoisseur Break rates
£185 per person April–October, £165 per person November 1999–March 2000 (Excludes 23–26 December and 30 December–2 January 2000)

A King Alfred's Connoisseur Break
With the thousandth anniversary of King Alfred, we are delighted to offer a special heritage treat. Arrive on Friday and enjoy the comforts of a feature room overlooking the cathedral, with a welcome gift of champagne and chocolates and a guidebook to the city and Winchester Trail. Savour dinner in the candlelit restaurant, followed by a complimentary liqueur with your coffee. On Saturday explore the city on a conducted walking tour, and in the afternoon visit the cathedral, returning to the hotel for a full traditional tea in the lounge. In the evening, dine to the sounds of the pianist in the restaurant. On your way home on

Sunday, visit the Wessex's sister hotel, The White Hart, and experience a traditional Sunday lunch in the city of Salisbury.

What's included in your break:
- 2 nights' dinner, bed and breakfast
- a welcome gift of champagne and chocolates
- a guidebook to the city and Winchester Trail
- 3-course dinner from the full à la carte menu (wine not included)
- full English breakfast both days
- conducted walking tour of Winchester
- full traditional tea (Saturday)
- traditional Sunday Lunch at the White Hart

Winchester

DRIVING ROUTE

Leave Winchester along the A31 to New Alresford, which is the start of the Watercress Line. Go south along the B3046, and turn left onto the A272. From here, take the A32, B2150 and A3 south to Portsmouth. Car and passenger ferries sail from Portsmouth to Fishbourne on the Isle of Wight. Osborne House and Cowes are on the A3021.

Town cryer outside Winchester Cathedral.

② Watercress Line

The area around the town of Alresford was once used to grow watercress, hence the quaint name of this equally charming steam railway, part of the Mid-Hants Railway. The ten-mile journey to Alton includes a four-course dinner at weekends.

③ HMS *Victory*

Immortalised in the Battle of Trafalgar (1805), Admiral Nelson's flagship, the HMS *Victory* is now docked permanently at Portsmouth. Other ships in the area include the 16th-century *Mary Rose*.

① Winchester Cathedral

The cathedral in this Roman city dates from 1079, but was not completed until the 14th century. Its most remarkable features are its nave – the longest in Europe – the crypt, which houses the tomb of St Swithun, and the marble font.

The HMS Victory at Portsmouth. A visit on board reveals the often harsh existence of life at sea in the 18th and 19th centuries.

④ Cowes

The Isle of Wight's northern town is generally the first sight most visitors see of the island. The town buzzes in the first week of August, when Cowes Week, the annual yachting festival, takes place.

⑤ Osborne House

This Italianate house, with ornate terraces and verandahs, was commissioned in 1845 by Prince Albert, to serve as the royal family's country home. Queen Victoria died here in 1901.

Heritage Hotels – Windermere
The Old England

Bowness-on-Windermere, Cumbria LA23 3DF See map page 10 Tel: (0)870 400 8130 Fax: (0)153 944 3432
Regional General Manager: Colin Campbell E-mail: HeritageHotels_Windermere.Old_England@forte-hotels.com

O n the shores of England's largest lake, the Old England boasts unrivalled views of Windermere. This elegant Victorian mansion, superbly furnished with fine antiques, is ideally situated for bustling Bowness. Enjoy a drink in the bar, then dinner in the candlelit Vinand Restaurant, which provides a panoramic view as well as fine fare. Gardens (with outdoor games of draughts) lead down to the hotel's own jetties. Beautiful scenery abounds in this treasured countryside, much of it preserved by the foresight of children's author Beatrix Potter, who invested her book earnings into buying parcels of land in the Lake District, ensuring its preservation when she endowed it to the National Trust.

Attractions: Outdoor Pool. Billiards.

Finest walking in the entire country found in the Lake District.

How to get there
The Old England is situated at the junction of the A5074 and the A592 on the shores of Windermere, about 18 miles from junction 36 of the M6.

Facilities: 72 bedrooms, 4 suites, hairdryer, trouser press, restaurant, bar, lounge, heated outdoor pool (May–September), billiard room, garden, hair salon, free car park.
Family: baby listening, baby-sitting.

Above and Below the Lake District rates
Price per person for two nights (based on two sharing)
May–October 1999
Fri/Sat–£200
Sun/Thur–£170
November 1999–April 2000
Fri/Sat–£170
Sun/Thur–£140
Lake view rooms supplement £15 per person per night
(Excludes 23–26 December and 30 December–2 January 2000)

Above and Below the Lake District
Situated on the shore of Lake Windermere, this elegant Victorian hotel commands unrivalled views of perhaps England's best-known and largest lake.

Bustling Bowness has many shops and includes the World of Beatrix Potter exhibition, while the jetties and the bay are just around the corner from the hotel.

On arrival there will be champagne and chocolates in your room. Dinner will be served to the accompaniment of the resident pianist, while you watch the activities on the lake until nightfall.

After breakfast you can board one of the Windermere Lake cruises, where you may venture to the small village of Ambleside. Stop here for a while and/or continue your journey back to Lakeside, where you will discover the Aquarium of the Lakes.

Meet the UK's largest collection of freshwater fish, including the predatory pike, encounter mischievous otters and meet sharks and rays from around the local coast. Not to be missed is the walk on Windermere's recreated lake bed to marvel at the diving ducks.

In the summer months the Lakeside and Haverthwaite steam train will take you on a journey through contrasting lake and river scenes of the Leven Valley.

Board one of the boats to return at your leisure to the hotel.

Back at the hotel dinner is served in the award-winning Vinand restaurant.

Breakfast prior to departure, then a last chance to explore before your journey home.

What's included in your break:
• 2 nights' dinner, bed and breakfast (wine not included)
• champagne and chocolates
• lake cruise to Ambleside
• entry to Aquarium of the Lakes
• return cruise on the Lake

Windermere

DRIVING ROUTE

Take the A592 from Windermere and cross the lake on the B5285 to Hill Top. Continue along this road to Coniston, then take the A593 north to Ambleside. Kendal lies to the southeast of Windermere on the A591.

Steamer on Lake Windermere.

1 Windermere

One of the most entertaining venues in this highly popular town is the Steamboat Museum, which exhibits old steamers formerly used to navigate the lakes. Cruises on Lake Windermere itself are still popular.

2 Hill Top

One of the many authors to gain inspiration from the region was Beatrix Potter, who used the country setting and wildlife around her in her beloved children's books. The house is now a museum, preserved as the author left it at the turn of the 20th century.

3 Coniston Water

The world speed record established in 1955 is one of the claims to fame of this quiet lake, but the driver Donald Campbell was killed when he tried to improve on his record in 1967. A memorial to the brave sportsman stands in the town.

4 Ambleside

The picturesque harbour on Lake Windermere makes an attractive stop-off point, where you can watch the many amateur sailors who moor their boats here.

5 Kendal

Regarded at the southern gateway to the Lake District, Kendal has remained true to its character as a working town rather than a tourist centre. Arthur Ransome, author of the children's classic *Swallows and Amazons,* worked in Kendal and is featured in the town's museum. Kendal is also known for its Kendal Mintcake, an extremely sugary peppermint flavoured snack.

The 13th-century church at Kendal.

Heritage Hotels – Windsor
The Castle Hotel

High Street, Windsor, Berks SL4 1LJ See map page 4 Tel: (0)870 400 8300. Fax: (0)175 383 0244
Regional General Manager: Jim Souter E-mail: HeritageHotels_Windsor.Castle@forte-hotels.com

Royal watchers get a bonus when they find out that this fine old Georgian hotel overlooks aspects of Windsor Castle and provides one of the finest views of the Changing of the Guard. Survey the dazzling ritual while taking morning coffee with teacakes or indulging in cream teas in the lounge. Of all the opulent bedrooms and superb suites, the most in-demand is the Ripley Suite, creaking with atmosphere, loaded with luxury and, be warned, booked far in advance.

Attractions: Royal rubber necking. Windsor Great Park. Royal Ascot. Theatre Royal for major theatrical events. Legoland. Excellent local shopping. Royal Station Arcade for notable fashion boutiques. Heathrow Airport in 25 minutes. 50 minutes direct rail to London.

How to get there
Leave the M4 at junction 6 and follow the signs for Windsor Castle. The hotel is in the High Street.

Facilities: 90 bedrooms, 4 four-posters, 3 suites, 14 executive rooms, 24-hour room service, hairdryer, trouser press, satellite TV, Castle Restaurant, the Grand Café, the Windsor Bar, the Pennington Lounge, free car park.
Family: baby listening, baby-sitting.

Special Break rates
May–November
£245 per person for two nights
December–April
£230 per person for two nights
Upgrade to suite
£40 per person for two nights
(Excludes 23–26 December and 30 December–2 January 2000)

Special Break
The Castle Hotel is located in the heart of our country's royal seat–Windsor.

Steeped in centuries of rich history, the Castle Hotel enjoys the ideal setting from which to discover all the town's attractions and shops.

On arrival at the Castle, settle into your superbly appointed bedroom prior to enjoying a welcome aperitif in the comfort of the Windsor Bar.

A sumptuous three-course dinner with coffee awaits you in the award-winning Castle Restaurant.

Enjoy a leisurely breakfast before you embark on a day discovering Windsor's rich royal history. From close to the castle's entrance the Good Friday Coach Tour will take you on an enjoyable and educational tour of Windsor and Eton.

Following a light lunch, it's a short walk across the way to discover the treasures of the world's largest and oldest inhabited castle.

On return to the Castle Hotel you will, no doubt, be ready to enjoy a splendid dinner and take a chance to recount the day's events.

No need to rush your departure – following breakfast take time to enjoy the many other treasures of this unique town.

What's included in your break:
- 2 nights' dinner, bed and breakfast (wine not included)
- aperitifs prior to dinner each evening
- first day lunch in the Grand Café
- Good Friday Guided Tour of Windsor
- entrance to Windsor Castle

Windsor

DRIVING ROUTE

Windsor Castle and St George's Chapel are in the centre of Windsor. To reach Frogmore House, go east along the A308 for one mile, and north along the B3021. Past Datchet, continue along the B3026 to Eton. Travel back south through Windsor along the A332 then B3022 to reach Legoland.

Windsor Castle, on the banks of the River Thames.

① Windsor Castle

A castle has stood on this site since Norman times, and the complex has developed over the years. Highlights of a tour around the castle are the Queen's Ballroom and the wonderfully ornate and technically brilliant Doll's House constructed for Queen Mary.

② St George's Chapel

Royalists will enjoy a tour of Windsor's chapel, where numerous monarchs are buried, including Henry VIII and Charles I, and its memorial for Prince Albert, erected by his grieving widow Queen Victoria.

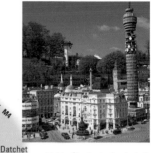

Models of London landmarks, built entirely out of Lego blocks, at Legoland.

③ Frogmore House

When King George III famously went mad, his long-suffering wife Queen Caroline was given Frogmore House as her own residence. Later, it was home to the mother of Queen Victoria, and both Victoria and her Prince Consort, Albert, are buried in the house's mausoleum.

④ Eton College

This exclusive public school was founded in 1440 and has educated numerous dignitaries and well-known names, who have all walked these picturesque streets in their obligatory black gowns. A museum in the college recounts the achievements of past students. Eton is once again in the public eye, as the chosen school of the Princes William and Harry.

⑤ Legoland

Set in Windsor Park, this entertaining park is given over to the great monuments of the world, built entirely out of Lego blocks. A popular attraction with children, who can tour the world at their own height.

Heritage Hotels – Woodstock
The Bear

Park Street, Woodstock OX20 1SZ See map page 4 Tel: (0)870 400 8202 Fax: (0)199 381 3380
Regional General Manager: Tony Marrinan E-mail: HeritageHotels_Woodstock.Bear@forte-hotels.com

One of old England's original 13th-century coaching inns, 15 minutes from Oxford. A romantic hideaway, at one time a retreat for Elizabeth Taylor and Richard Burton during their long on-off love affair. Candlelight, oak beams, open fireplaces and dishes from around the world are served in the restaurant.

Attractions: Local leisure facilities. A stone's throw from Blenheim Palace, birthplace of Sir William Churchill, who is buried at nearby Bladon. Capability Brown created the magical gardens and the lake at Blenheim. Charming covered market — eclectic items from prints to poultry. Bookshops. Antiques. Handy for Stratford-upon-Avon and the Cotswolds, reachable within the hour.

How to get there
The Bear can be found beside the Town Hall, on Park Street, just off the High Street in the centre of Woodstock.

Facilities: 44 bedrooms, 3 four-posters, 1 suite, hairdryer, trouser press, David Garrick restaurant (AA Rosette), bistro, cocktail bar, lounge, open fires in winter, free parking (limited).
Family: baby listening, baby-sitting.

Romantic Hideaway Break rates
Validity dates: all dates until March 2000
Mid-week
£220 per person for two nights
Weekends
£240 per person for two nights
Upgrade to a suite or four-poster room — £50 per person, for two nights
(all rates apply to two people sharing, wine not included with meals)
(Excludes 23–26 December and 30 December–2 January 2000)

Romantic Hideaway Break
Dating back to the 13th century, the Bear at Woodstock is the ideal romantic hideaway hotel. Each of the bedrooms is full of character, with such features as fireplaces, oak beams and antiques. (Richard Burton proposed to Elizabeth Taylor the second time in the Marlborough Suite!)

The oak-beamed restaurant is candlelit every evening, while the tavern-style bar is a lovely place to have afternoon tea or just sit and read a book.

For our Romantic Hideaway Break, chocolates, flowers and champagne await you in your room on your first evening. Enjoy a glass of champagne before dinner in the restaurant and finish your meal with a liqueur of your choice.

The next morning, after a hearty English breakfast, you can join a walking tour of Royal Woodstock (weekends only). You will also be issued with free entry to Blenheim Palace, the home of the Duke of Marlborough (available only until the end of October – although the gardens designed by Capability Brown are open throughout the year). The Palace is only three minutes' walk from the hotel.

Enjoy dinner in the restaurant that evening with champagne and liqueurs and retire to either your courtyard room or upstairs in the hotel.

After breakfast the next morning you may want another stroll through Woodstock or drive to nearby Oxford (15 minutes).

What's included in your break:
- 2 nights' dinner, bed and breakfast
- bathrobes, chocolates, champagne and flowers in the room on arrival
- a glass of champagne before dinner each evening and a liqueur to follow
- 2 full English breakfasts
- walking tour of Royal Woodstock (weekends)
- entrance to Blenheim Palace

Woodstock

DRIVING ROUTE

Blenheim Palace is one mile outside of Woodstock on the A44. Return to Woodstock and take the B4437 and A424 to Bourton-on-the-Water, then take the A429 on to Stow-on-the-Wold. Take the A436 and A44 to Chipping Norton, then to Enstone, joining the B4030 eastwards to Bicester.

② Bourton-on-the-Water

A charming Cotswolds village, Bourton's beauty lies in its many miniature ornamental bridges, crossing the River Windrush, which flows through the town. A miniature model village showing the great buildings of the world is popular with children.

① Blenheim Palace

Queen Anne commissioned this baroque palace for the first Duke of Marlborough as a reward for his victory over the French in the Battle of Blenheim in 1704. Designed by John Vanbrugh, the palace was completed in 1722 and includes landscaped gardens and a lake. In 1874, the palace was the birthplace of Sir Winston Churchill.

The magnificent Blenheim Palace was the birthplace of the former British prime minister, Sir Winston Churchill.

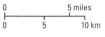

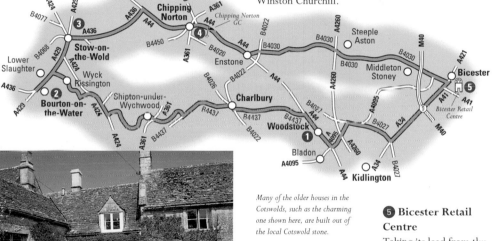

Many of the older houses in the Cotswolds, such as the charming one shown here, are built out of the local Cotswold stone.

④ Chipping Norton

Having largely escaped the mass tourism of its neighbouring towns and villages, Chipping Norton is nevertheless worth a visit, particularly for its 17th-century almshouses and its old Tweed Mill, now converted into luxury homes.

③ Stow-on-the-Wold

Stow is unique for its many narrow lanes, which all flow into the central market square – they were apparently designed so that sheep could be herded to market more easily. Today the lanes are lined with souvenir and antique shops.

⑤ Bicester Retail Centre

Taking its lead from the outlet centres across the United States, Bicester Retail Centre is Britain's first cut-price shopping "village". All clothes, ranging from designer names to high street stores, are on sale at half their original price.

Heritage Hotels – Worcester
The Giffard

High Street, Worcester WR1 2QR. See map page 7 Tel: (0)870 400 8133 Fax: (0)190 572 3458
Regional General Manager: James Lever E-mail: HeritageHotels_Giffard.Worcester@forte-hotels.com

Situated opposite the magnificent 11th-century Worcester Cathedral, which holds many events throughout the year, the Giffard is a perfect choice for those exploring Worcester, a city well known for its county cricket ground and horse-racing. Round off a wonderful day at the races in the bar. Nearby are the imposing Malvern Hills that so inspired the music of Sir Edward Elgar. Visit at apple blossom time and incorporate a visit to the Vale of Evesham.

How to get there
From Junction 7 on the M5, head for the city centre, going through 3 sets of traffic lights. After the third set keep in the right hand lane. Turn right around the island opposite the Cathedral. The Giffard hotel is on your left. Park in the NCP adjacent to the hotel.

Facilities: 103 bedrooms, restaurant, 2 bars, free car park
Family: baby listening

Attractions: A tour of the Royal Worcester Porcelain Factory. Fine river walks. Good shopping. Malvern Hills. The Vale of Evesham. Stratford. Cheltenham. Safari Park at Bewdley.

Special Break rates
April–October
Mid-week–£190
Weekend–£180
November–March
Mid-week – £180
Weekend – £180
Prices are per person for two nights with all activities mentioned included. (Excludes 22–28 August, 23–27 December and 30 December–2 January 2000)

Special Break
Check in to the hotel from 2pm and enjoy an afternoon cream tea at your leisure. Relax before a 3-course dinner with a half-bottle of house wine per person, then why not stroll down to the river and enjoy the views.

After breakfast the following day visit the world-famous Royal Worcester Porcelain Factory then return to the hotel for a leisurely lunch.

In the afternoon visit the Commandary Museum depicting the English Civil Wars and its fascinating history.

Return to the Giffard to freshen up before a glass of chilled wine or sherry in the hotel's cocktail bar followed by a farewell 3-course dinner.

After breakfast the next morning collect your complimentary porcelain gift before visiting the fine shopping centres prior to your journey home.

What's included in your break:
• 2 nights' dinner, bed and breakfast
• 3-course dinner (half-bottle of house wine per person included)
• English breakfast
• visit to the Royal Worcester Porcelain Factory
• lunch (day 2)
• visit to the Commandary Museum
• glass of sherry at the bar (day 2)
• a porcelain gift

Worcester

DRIVING ROUTE

The A449 and A4025 leads from Worcester to Stourport-on-Severn and the start of the Severn Valley Railway at Bewdley. Take the A458 and the A491 to Dudley. Take the B4176 towards Telford, and turn left to Ironbridge. Continue south along the A4169 to reach Much Wenlock.

The platform at Highley Station, on the Severn Valley Railway route.

The Ironbridge, over the River Severn is thought to be the world's first iron bridge.

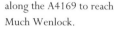

④ Ironbridge

The Ironbridge Gorge Museum has been so successful at capturing the region's past in a complex spreading over six miles that it has become a UNESCO World Heritage Site. Various areas detail the many industries and crafts that thrived in the region, including an open-air museum where you can "walk through" 19th-century life.

① Worcester

The most dominating feature of the city is its 10th-century cathedral, but there are also two interesting museums: a porcelain museum detailing the city's well-known industry; and the former home of Edward Elgar, one of England's finest composers.

② Severn Valley Railway

This preserved steam railway runs a 16-mile route from Kidderminster to Bridgenorth along the path of the River Severn. Dating from 1862, the line was primarily used for transport of goods in the region, but today it has been preserved purely for the enjoyment of tourists.

③ Black Country

Those interested in industrial heritage should pay a visit to this small region of England, so named for its working past, notably the mining of coal. Dudley is the best stopping-off point, not least for its museum, which details the area's history with reconstructed homes, factories and staff dressed in period costume.

⑤ Much Wenlock

In contrast to the working nature of much of this region, Much Wenlock has preserved its quiet village atmosphere, in existence since Elizabethan times. Wenlock Edge is a popular place for ramblers, with its wonderful views across to Wales.

Ullswater, Leeming House

Heritage Hotels Website

We combine the best of our timeless hospitality with up to the minute information for all of your travel needs. Click into information on local events, places of interest, historic houses and museums, then book the Heritage Hotel of your choice.

www.heritage-hotels.com

Break Away to Heritage

The following abbreviations are used throughout this booklet:
BB – bed & breakfast,
DBB – dinner, bed & breakfast,
PP – per person,
SO – sole occupancy supplement

There's no better way to recharge your batteries than on a relaxing Heritage Hotels leisure break. With 47 Heritage Hotels ideally located throughout the UK, there's no shortage of highly individual venues to choose from. Enjoy excellent amenities, exceptional service and an inviting range of breaks at very attractive rates throughout the year.

Breaks start from just £30 per person per night

An exciting range to meet all needs

Choose from a broad range of breaks to suit your requirements and budget.

- **Midweek Leisure Break**
  One or more consecutive nights between Monday–Thursday. Prices from £30 per person per night.
- **Weekend Leisure Break**
  One or more consecutive nights between Friday–Sunday inclusive (includes Bank Holiday Mondays).
  Prices from £30 per person per night.
- **Half-price Sunday nights**
  Book a weekend break (to include Friday and Saturday night) on bed & breakfast or dinner, bed & breakfast basis and you stay on Sunday night for 50% of the weekend leisure break price.
  Prices from £75 per person for the weekend.
- **Weekaways bed & breakfast package**
  Stay 5 nights or more on a bed & breakfast basis and receive a considerable discount on standard bed & breakfast rates.
  Prices from £115 per person for a 5 night stay.

Special Heritage Breaks (available at selected hotels)

During the rest of 1999 and early 2000, Heritage special breaks at selected hotels include:

- "Music at Leisure". See page 12. Prices from £235.
- "Break for Murder". See page 14. Prices from £190.
- Christmas '99. See page 131. Prices from £295.
- Millennium Breaks. See page 131. Prices from £325.

St Andrews, Rusacks

Christmas '99 & Millennium Packages

Traditional Christmas

Comprehensive Package includes:
• 3 nights' accommodation from 24-26 December, • Welcome reception on Christmas Eve • Full traditional breakfast each morning • Minimum 3 course dinner or buffet each evening • Morning coffee & afternoon tea each day • Welcome drink on return from Midnight Mass • Traditional 4 course lunch on Christmas Day • Visit from Santa Claus on Christmas Day • Local entertainment such as bell ringers, pantomime, carol singers • Details of local places of interest open during the period • Boxing Day buffet or 3 course lunch • Boxing Day 3 course dinner and entertainment

Peace & Quiet Christmas

Comprehensive Package includes:
• 3 nights' accommodation from 24-26 December • Welcome reception on Christmas Eve • Full traditional breakfast each morning • Minimum 3 course dinner or buffet each evening • Morning coffee & afternoon tea each day • Traditional 4 course lunch on Christmas Day • Introduction to local places of interest open during the period • Boxing Day buffet or 3 course lunch • Boxing Day 3 course dinner

Millennium Celebration

Welcome 2000 in champagne style. Join us in a momentous Millennium Celebration in one of our ideally placed hotels up and down the country. We'll lay on everything you could possibly need, so all you have to do is relax and enjoy the time of your life along with your family, partner or friends. It's the perfect way to mark a truly historic occasion.
Comprehensive Package includes:
Accommodation • Champagne Reception • New Year's Eve Dinner • Traditional celebrations at midnight • Fireworks at selected hotels • Full traditional breakfast

Millennium House Party

For the night of a lifetime, what could be more appropriate than a party to match? Want to hold your own party and know everything is taken care of? Take over any one of 11 Heritage Hotels with your friends and family and we can tailor make the celebrations for you. Our intimate hotels provide the perfect setting to see in a new era and guaranteed high levels of service mean you can step back, relax and enjoy your own exclusive Millennium House Party. Packages vary by hotel, but most include
• Accommodation (3 nights) • Food and service • Tailor-made options
• Entertainment can be arranged to your specifications

Visiting Friends & Relatives

If you're planning a pre- or post-holiday visit to friends or relatives, there's a conveniently-located Heritage Hotel just waiting to welcome you. Our special 'friends and relatives' rates include accommodation and full traditional breakfast and are available only on the following dates:

17-23 December 1999 • 27-29 December 1999 • 02-09 January 2000

Make your Christmas or Millennium celebrations truly memorable. Our tailor-made festive breaks not only offer the perfect blend of customary Heritage hospitality and exemplary service, but also an exciting choice of packages and entertainment that cater for all. So relax, and leave all the usual holiday hassles far behind.

For a copy of our Christmas & Millennium Celebrations brochure please call 0345 700 350 quoting 'MH1'.

Prices - What's Included

• Twin/double room (or single room for single guests) with colour TV, tea and coffee making facilities, direct dial telephone, en suite bathroom

• Either bed & breakfast (prices from £30 per person per night) including continental or full traditional breakfast each morning
or

• dinner, bed & breakfast (prices from £45 per person per night) including continental or full traditional breakfast each morning and a 3-course dinner with tea or coffee

• Prices are in £'s per person sharing a twin/double room, or for one person in a single room unless otherwise stated

Single guests are charged standard rates, though if no single room is available a sole occupancy supplement may apply

How to use this price guide
Pages 133–137 detail the prices for all hotels for the period 1 April 1999–31 March 2000. To find a particular price, select the month, whether you will be going midweek or at the weekend and whether you would like dinner included in your package. Then just go down the column until you reach the hotel of your choice.

Marlow, Compleat Angler

Location	Hotel	June 1999										July 1999										
		Midweek				Weekend				Weekaway		Midweek				Weekend				Weekaway	
		BB		DBB		BB		DBB		5 days or more BB		BB		DBB		BB		DBB		5 days or more BB	
		PP	SO	PP	SO	PP	SO	PP	SO	PP	SO	PP	SO	PP	SO	PP	SO	PP	SO	PP	SO
Abingdon	The Upper Reaches	67	20	82	20	67	25	82	25	60	20	67	20	82	20	67	25	82	25	60	20
Alfriston	The Star Inn	56	20	70	20	66	20	80	20	53	20	56	20	70	20	66	20	80	20	53	20
Amersham	The Crown	80	50	100	50	50	20	68	20	-	-	80	50	100	50	50	20	68	20	-	-
Ascot	The Berystede	85	50	99	20	55	20	70	20	-	-	75	50	89	20	55	20	70	20	-	-
Banbury	Whately Hall	50	40	65	40	35	15	50	10	40	40	45	40	60	40	35	15	50	10	37	40
Bath	The Francis	59	20	79	20	59	20	79	20	56	20	54	20	74	20	54	20	74	20	47	20
Bath	The Bath Spa	80	20	100	20	119	20	139	20	87	20	75	20	95	20	109	20	129	20	81	20
Box Hill	The Burford Bridge	85	50	99	50	49	20	59	20	-	-	75	50	89	20	49	20	59	20	-	-
Camberley	Frimley Hall	85	50	99	50	39	20	49	20	-	-	75	50	89	50	39	20	49	20	-	-
Canterbury	The Chaucer Hotel	56	30	66	30	55	30	65	30	48	30	56	30	66	30	60	30	70	30	50	30
Cheltenham	The Queen's	65	30	80	30	50	20	65	20	52	40	55	30	70	50	50	20	65	20	42	40
Chester	Blossoms Hotel	50	30	65	30	50	20	65	20	43	30	50	30	65	30	50	20	65	20	43	30
Coventry	Brandon Hall	55	50	70	50	40	15	55	15	40	50	55	50	70	50	40	15	55	15	40	50
Dartmouth	The Dart Marina	64	25	85	25	64	25	85	25	57	25	64	25	85	25	64	25	85	25	57	25
Dorking	The White Horse	62	50	82	50	39	20	49	20	-	-	52	50	72	50	39	20	49	20	-	-
Dovedale	The Peveril of the Peak	47	10	62	10	47	10	62	10	40	10	53	10	68	10	53	10	68	10	46	10
Dunster	The Luttrell Arms	55	0	65	0	55	0	65	0	48	10	55	0	65	0	55	0	65	0	48	10
Exeter	The Southgate	55	30	65	30	45	20	55	20	49	30	55	30	65	30	50	20	60	20	43	30
Farnham	The Bush Hotel	77	50	97	50	39	20	49	20	-	-	77	50	97	50	39	20	49	20	-	-
Grasmere	The Swan	54	10	69	10	67	20	82	20	52	20	54	10	69	10	67	20	82	20	52	20
Helmsley	The Black Swan	55	20	75	20	78	20	98	20	58	20	55	20	75	20	78	20	98	20	58	20
Hereford	The Green Dragon	42	20	58	20	42	20	58	20	35	20	45	20	59	20	45	20	59	20	38	20
Hertingfordbury	The White Horse	65	40	80	40	45	0	60	0	50	40	54	40	65	40	45	0	60	0	50	40
Kingston	Kingston Lodge	80	50	95	50	50	20	65	20	-	-	80	50	95	50	50	20	65	20	-	-
Lavenham	The Swan	70	20	80	20	75	20	85	20	65	20	70	20	80	20	75	20	85	20	65	20
Lincoln	The White Hart	59	20	65	20	59	20	65	20	53	45	49	20	59	20	49	20	59	20	43	45
Marlborough	The Castle & Ball	35	20	50	20	35	15	50	15	27	20	35	20	50	20	35	15	50	15	27	20
Marlow	The Compleat Angler	100	60	115	60	80	25	100	25	84	60	100	60	115	60	80	25	100	25	84	60
Matlock	The New Bath Hotel	54	10	64	10	54	10	64	10	47	10	59	10	69	10	59	10	69	10	52	10
Mudeford	Avonmouth Hotel	-	20	64	20	64	20	69	20	50	20	-	20	79	20	74	20	79	20	53	20
North Berwick	The Marine	60	10	75	10	60	0	75	0	53	10	60	10	75	10	60	0	75	0	53	10
Oxford	Eastgate Hotel	65	25	80	25	65	25	80	25	58	30	55	25	70	25	55	25	70	25	48	30
Oxford	The Randolph	78	40	93	40	78	40	93	40	71	40	78	40	93	40	78	40	93	40	71	40
Padstow	The Metropole	55	20	69	20	55	20	69	20	50	20	60	20	79	20	-	20	79	20	57	20
Romsey	The White Horse	40	25	50	25	35	20	50	20	31	20	40	25	50	25	35	20	50	20	31	20
Ross on Wye	The Royal	52	10	63	10	52	10	63	10	40	10	55	10	65	10	55	10	65	10	42	10
St.Andrews	Rusacks Hotel	99	15	119	15	99	15	119	15	90	35	99	15	119	15	99	15	119	15	90	35
Salisbury	The White Hart	65	15	80	15	58	15	73	15	55	15	60	15	75	15	53	15	68	15	50	15
Sherborne	The Sherborne	35	15	50	15	35	15	50	15	27	15	35	15	50	15	35	15	50	15	27	15
Staines	The Thames Lodge	80	50	95	50	40	10	55	10	-	-	80	50	95	50	40	10	55	10	-	-
Stratford-upon-Avon	The Alveston Manor	79	20	99	20	74	20	89	20	70	20	65	20	84	20	69	20	84	20	62	20
Stratford-upon-Avon	The Shakespeare	84	30	105	30	84	30	99	30	77	30	79	30	94	30	84	30	94	30	75	30
Stratford-upon-Avon	The Swan's Nest	69	20	84	20	N/A	20	79	20	62	20	59	20	74	20	59	20	74	20	52	20
Ullswater	Leeming House	70	20	90	20	100	20	120	20	76	20	70	20	90	20	100	20	120	20	76	20
Winchester	The Wessex	64	50	79	50	54	20	69	20	53	20	54	50	69	50	49	20	64	20	45	20
Windermere	The Old England	55	20	70	20	70	20	85	20	54	20	55	20	70	20	70	20	85	20	54	20
Windsor	The Castle Hotel	85	50	99	50	75	20	90	20	-	-	75	50	89	50	75	20	90	20	-	-
Woodstock	The Bear	65	30	80	30	70	30	87	30	60	30	62	30	77	30	67	30	84	30	60	30
Worcester	The Giffard	42	0	54	0	38	0	49	0	33	10	42	0	54	0	38	0	49	0	33	10

KEY: BB – Bed & Breakfast   DBB – Dinner, Bed & Breakfast   PP – Per Person   SO – Sole Occupancy Supplement

For more information look on www.heritage-hotels.com or call 0345 404040

133

Location	Hotel	August 1999 Midweek BB		August 1999 Midweek DBB		August 1999 Weekend BB		August 1999 Weekend DBB		August 1999 Weekaway 5 days or more BB		September 1999 Midweek BB		September 1999 Midweek DBB		September 1999 Weekend BB		September 1999 Weekend DBB		September 1999 Weekaway 5 days or more BB	
		PP	SO	PP	SO	PP	SO	PP	SO	PP	SO	PP	SO	PP	SO	PP	SO	PP	SO	PP	SO
Abingdon	The Upper Reaches	67	20	82	20	67	25	82	25	60	20	67	20	82	20	67	25	82	25	60	20
Alfriston	The Star Inn	56	20	70	20	66	20	80	20	53	20	56	20	70	20	66	20	80	20	53	20
Amersham	The Crown	80	50	100	50	50	20	68	20	-	-	80	50	100	50	50	20	68	20	-	-
Ascot	The Berystede	75	50	89	20	55	20	70	20	-	-	85	50	89	20	55	20	70	20	-	-
Banbury	Whately Hall	45	40	60	40	35	15	50	10	37	40	50	40	65	40	40	15	55	10	37	40
Bath	The Francis	49	20	69	20	54	20	74	20	45	20	49	20	69	20	54	20	74	20	45	20
Bath	The Bath Spa	60	20	80	20	104	20	124	20	70	20	60	20	80	20	109	20	129	20	70	20
Box Hill	The Burford Bridge	75	50	89	50	49	20	59	20	-	-	85	50	99	50	49	20	59	20	-	-
Camberley	Frimley Hall	75	50	89	50	39	20	49	20	-	-	85	50	99	50	39	20	49	20	-	-
Canterbury	The Chaucer Hotel	56	30	66	30	60	30	70	30	50	30	56	30	66	30	60	30	70	30	50	30
Cheltenham	The Queen's	55	30	70	50	50	20	55	20	52	40	65	30	80	50	50	20	65	20	52	40
Chester	Blossoms Hotel	50	30	65	30	50	20	65	20	43	30	50	30	65	30	50	20	65	20	43	30
Coventry	Brandon Hall	35	50	50	50	35	15	50	15	28	50	55	50	70	50	35	15	50	15	40	50
Dartmouth	The Dart Marina	64	25	85	25	64	25	85	25	57	25	64	25	85	25	64	25	85	25	57	25
Dorking	The White Horse	52	50	72	50	39	20	49	20	-	-	62	50	82	50	39	20	49	20	-	-
Dovedale	The Peveril of the Peak	53	10	68	10	53	10	68	10	46	10	47	10	62	10	47	10	62	10	40	10
Dunster	The Luttrell Arms	55	0	65	0	55	0	65	0	48	10	55	0	65	0	55	0	65	0	48	10
Exeter	The Southgate	55	30	65	30	50	20	60	20	43	30	55	30	65	30	50	20	60	20	43	30
Farnham	The Bush Hotel	77	50	97	50	39	20	49	20	-	-	87	50	107	50	39	20	49	20	-	-
Grasmere	The Swan	54	10	69	10	67	20	82	20	52	20	54	10	69	10	67	20	82	20	52	20
Helmsley	The Black Swan	70	20	90	20	85	20	105	20	70	20	75	20	95	20	88	20	108	20	70	20
Hereford	The Green Dragon	45	20	59	20	45	20	59	20	38	20	45	20	59	20	45	20	59	20	38	20
Hertingfordbury	The White Horse	50	40	65	40	45	0	60	0	42	40	65	40	80	40	45	0	60	0	42	40
Kingston	Kingston Lodge	60	50	75	50	50	20	65	20	-	-	80	50	95	50	50	20	65	20	-	-
Lavenham	The Swan	70	20	80	20	75	20	85	20	65	20	67	20	77	20	67	20	77	20	60	20
Lincoln	The White Hart	49	20	59	20	49	20	59	20	43	45	59	20	65	20	59	20	65	20	53	45
Marlborough	The Castle & Ball	35	20	50	20	35	15	50	15	27	20	35	20	50	20	35	15	50	15	27	20
Marlow	The Compleat Angler	70	60	85	60	80	25	100	25	69	60	100	60	115	60	80	25	100	25	84	60
Matlock	The New Bath Hotel	59	10	69	10	59	10	69	10	52	10	54	10	64	10	54	10	64	10	47	10
Mudeford	Avonmouth Hotel	-	20	79	20	74	20	79	20	53	20	-	20	79	20	74	20	79	20	53	20
North Berwick	The Marine	60	10	75	10	60	0	75	0	53	10	55	10	70	10	55	0	70	0	48	10
Oxford	Eastgate Hotel	55	25	70	25	55	25	70	25	48	30	65	25	80	25	65	25	80	25	58	30
Oxford	The Randolph	60	40	75	40	60	40	75	40	53	40	78	40	93	40	78	40	93	40	71	40
Padstow	The Metropole	65	20	84	20	-	20	84	20	60	20	60	20	79	20	-	20	79	20	57	20
Romsey	The White Horse	35	25	50	25	35	20	50	20	27	20	35	25	50	25	35	20	50	20	27	20
Ross on Wye	The Royal	55	10	65	10	55	10	65	10	42	10	55	10	65	10	55	10	65	10	42	10
St.Andrews	Rusacks Hotel	99	15	119	15	99	15	119	15	90	35	88	15	108	15	88	15	108	15	80	35
Salisbury	The White Hart	60	15	75	15	53	15	68	15	50	15	65	15	80	15	60	15	75	15	55	15
Sherborne	The Sherborne	35	15	50	15	35	15	50	15	27	15	35	15	50	15	35	15	50	15	27	15
Staines	The Thames Lodge	75	50	90	50	40	10	55	10	-	-	80	50	95	50	40	10	55	10	-	-
Stratford-upon-Avon	The Alveston Manor	65	20	84	20	65	20	84	20	62	20	79	20	99	20	74	20	89	20	70	20
Stratford-upon-Avon	The Shakespeare	79	30	94	30	79	30	94	30	72	30	84	30	105	30	84	30	99	30	77	30
Stratford-upon-Avon	The Swan's Nest	59	20	74	20	59	20	74	20	52	20	69	20	84	20	N/A	20	79	20	72	20
Ullswater	Leeming House	70	20	90	20	100	20	120	20	76	20	70	20	90	20	100	20	120	20	76	20
Winchester	The Wessex	54	50	69	50	49	20	64	20	45	50	64	50	79	50	54	20	69	20	53	50
Windermere	The Old England	55	20	70	20	70	20	85	20	54	20	55	20	70	20	70	20	85	20	54	20
Windsor	The Castle Hotel	75	50	89	50	75	20	90	20	-	-	85	50	99	50	55	20	70	20	-	-
Woodstock	The Bear	55	30	70	30	61	30	76	30	50	30	65	30	80	30	70	30	87	30	60	30
Worcester	The Giffard	38	0	49	0	38	0	49	0	33	10	42	0	54	0	42	0	54	0	35	10

KEY: BB – Bed & Breakfast   DBB – Dinner, Bed & Breakfast   PP – Per Person   SO – Sole Occupancy Supplement

For more information look on www.heritage-hotels.com or call 0345 404040

Location	Hotel	October 1999 Midweek BB PP	SO	DBB PP	SO	October 1999 Weekend BB PP	SO	DBB PP	SO	October 1999 Weekaway 5 days or more BB PP	SO	November 1999 Midweek BB PP	SO	DBB PP	SO	November 1999 Weekend BB PP	SO	DBB PP	SO	November 1999 Weekaway 5 days or more BB PP	SO
Abingdon	The Upper Reaches	67	20	82	20	67	25	82	25	60	20	56	20	71	20	56	25	71	25	49	20
Alfriston	The Star Inn	45	20	62	20	49	20	66	20	40	20	45	20	62	20	49	20	66	20	40	20
Amersham	The Crown	80	50	100	50	48	20	65	20	-	-	80	50	100	50	48	20	62	20	-	-
Ascot	The Berystede	85	50	99	20	55	20	70	20	-	-	85	50	99	20	55	20	70	20	-	-
Banbury	Whately Hall	50	40	65	40	40	15	55	10	40	40	50	40	65	40	35	15	50	10	40	40
Bath	The Francis	54	20	74	20	59	20	79	20	49	20	44	20	59	20	49	20	69	20	39	20
Bath	The Bath Spa	75	20	95	20	119	20	159	20	81	20	55	20	65	20	99	20	119	20	65	20
Box Hill	The Burford Bridge	85	50	99	50	49	20	59	20	-	-	85	50	99	50	49	20	59	20	-	-
Camberley	Frimley Hall	85	50	99	50	39	20	49	20	-	-	85	50	99	50	39	20	49	20	-	-
Canterbury	The Chaucer Hotel	53	30	63	30	55	30	65	30	45	30	49	30	59	30	49	30	59	30	42	30
Cheltenham	The Queen's	65	30	80	50	50	20	65	20	52	40	65	30	80	50	50	20	65	20	52	40
Chester	Blossoms Hotel	45	30	60	30	45	20	60	20	38	30	40	30	55	30	40	20	55	20	33	30
Coventry	Brandon Hall	55	50	70	50	35	15	50	15	40	50	55	50	70	50	35	15	50	15	40	50
Dartmouth	The Dart Marina	64	25	75	25	64	25	75	25	57	25	44	25	59	25	44	25	59	25	37	25
Dorking	The White Horse	62	50	82	50	39	20	49	20	-	-	62	50	82	50	39	20	49	20	-	-
Dovedale	The Peveril of the Peak	47	10	62	10	47	10	62	10	40	10	42	10	57	10	42	10	57	10	35	10
Dunster	The Luttrell Arms	45	0	55	0	45	0	55	0	38	10	40	0	45	0	40	0	55	0	33	10
Exeter	The Southgate	55	30	65	30	50	20	60	20	43	30	50	30	70	30	50	20	55	20	43	30
Farnham	The Bush Hotel	87	50	107	50	39	20	49	20	-	-	87	50	107	50	39	20	49	20	-	-
Grasmere	The Swan	54	10	69	10	67	20	82	20	52	20	44	10	59	10	57	20	72	20	42	20
Helmsley	The Black Swan	75	20	95	20	88	20	108	20	70	20	45	20	65	20	60	20	80	20	48	20
Hereford	The Green Dragon	42	20	58	20	42	20	58	20	35	20	35	20	49	20	35	20	49	20	28	20
Hertingfordbury	The White Horse	65	40	80	40	45	0	60	0	50	40	65	40	80	40	42	0	54	0	48	40
Kingston	Kingston Lodge	80	50	95	50	40	20	55	20	-	-	80	50	95	50	40	20	55	20	-	-
Lavenham	The Swan	67	20	77	20	67	20	77	20	60	20	54	20	64	20	60	20	70	20	49	20
Lincoln	The White Hart	59	20	65	20	59	20	65	20	53	45	49	20	59	20	49	20	59	20	43	45
Marlborough	The Castle & Ball	35	20	45	20	35	15	45	15	27	20	32	20	45	20	30	15	45	15	25	20
Marlow	The Compleat Angler	100	60	115	60	80	25	100	25	84	60	75	60	90	60	70	25	90	25	65	60
Matlock	The New Bath Hotel	54	10	64	10	54	10	64	10	47	10	49	10	59	10	49	10	59	10	42	10
Mudeford	Avonmouth Hotel	59	20	64	20	64	20	69	20	50	20	40	20	54	20	45	20	59	20	40	20
North Berwick	The Marine	55	10	70	10	55	0	70	0	48	10	42	10	57	10	42	0	57	0	35	10
Oxford	Eastgate Hotel	65	25	80	25	65	25	80	25	58	30	65	25	80	25	65	25	80	25	58	30
Oxford	The Randolph	78	40	93	40	78	40	93	40	71	40	78	40	93	40	78	40	93	40	71	40
Padstow	The Metropole	55	20	69	20	55	20	69	20	50	20	40	20	49	20	40	20	49	20	35	20
Romsey	The White Horse	30	25	45	25	30	20	45	20	23	20	30	25	45	25	30	20	45	20	23	20
Ross on Wye	The Royal	52	10	63	10	52	10	63	10	40	10	45	10	57	10	45	10	57	10	38	10
St.Andrews	Rusacks Hotel	88	15	108	15	88	15	108	15	80	35	50	15	65	15	50	15	65	15	42	35
Salisbury	The White Hart	65	15	80	15	60	15	75	15	55	15	60	15	75	15	53	15	68	15	50	15
Sherborne	The Sherborne	35	15	50	15	35	15	50	15	27	15	30	15	40	15	30	15	40	15	23	15
Staines	Thames Lodge	80	50	95	50	40	10	55	10	-	-	80	50	95	50	40	10	55	10	-	-
Stratford upon Avon	The Alveston Manor	79	20	99	20	74	20	89	20	70	20	65	20	80	20	69	20	80	20	60	20
Stratford-upon-Avon	The Shakespeare	84	30	105	30	84	30	99	30	77	30	79	30	94	30	79	30	94	30	72	30
Stratford-upon-Avon	The Swan's Nest	69	20	84	20	N/A	20	79	20	62	20	59	20	74	20	59	20	74	20	52	20
Ullswater	Leeming House	70	20	90	20	100	20	120	20	76	20	50	20	70	20	80	20	100	20	57	20
Winchester	The Wessex	64	50	79	50	54	20	69	20	53	20	54	50	69	50	49	20	64	20	45	20
Windermere	The Old England	55	20	70	20	70	20	85	20	54	20	39	20	54	20	54	20	69	20	37	20
Windsor	The Castle Hotel	85	50	99	50	55	20	70	20	-	-	85	50	99	50	55	20	70	20	-	-
Woodstock	The Bear	65	30	80	30	70	30	87	30	60	30	55	30	70	30	61	30	76	30	50	30
Worcester	The Giffard	42	0	54	0	42	0	54	0	35	10	35	0	47	0	35	0	47	0	28	10

KEY: BB – Bed & Breakfast   DBB – Dinner, Bed & Breakfast   PP – Per Person   SO – Sole Occupancy Supplement

For more information look on www.heritage-hotels.com or call 0345 404040

Location	Hotel	December 1999†										January 2000#									
		Midweek				Weekend				Weekaway		Midweek				Weekend				Weekaway	
		BB		DBB		BB		DBB		5 days or more BB		BB		DBB		BB		DBB		5 days or more BB	
		PP	SO	PP	SO	PP	SO	PP	SO	PP	SO	PP	SO	PP	SO	PP	SO	PP	SO	PP	SO
Abingdon	The Upper Reaches	56	20	71	20	56	25	71	25	49	20	56	20	71	20	56	25	71	25	49	20
Alfriston	The Star Inn	45	20	62	20	49	20	66	20	40	20	39	20	56	20	40	20	54	20	32	20
Amersham	The Crown	80	50	100	50	46	20	62	20	-	-	80	50	100	50	45	20	60	20	-	-
Ascot	The Berystede	95	50	89	20	55	20	70	20	-	-	85	50	99	20	49	20	65	20	-	-
Banbury	Whately Hall	45	40	60	40	35	15	50	10	34	40	45	40	60	40	35	15	50	10	34	40
Bath	The Francis	39	20	59	20	49	20	69	20	37	20	39	20	59	20	54	20	44	20	37	20
Bath	The Bath Spa	45	20	65	20	99	20	119	20	59	20	45	20	65	20	99	20	119	20	59	20
Box Hill	The Burford Bridge	75	50	89	50	49	20	59	20	-	-	85	50	99	50	49	20	59	20	-	-
Camberley	Frimley Hall	75	50	89	50	39	20	49	20	-	-	85	50	99	50	39	20	49	20	-	-
Canterbury	The Chaucer Hotel	45	30	55	30	45	30	55	30	37	30	45	30	55	30	45	30	55	30	37	30
Cheltenham	The Queen's	55	30	70	50	40	20	55	20	45	40	55	30	70	50	40	20	55	20	40	40
Chester	Blossoms Hotel	35	30	50	30	35	20	50	20	28	30	35	30	50	30	35	20	50	20	28	30
Coventry	Brandon Hall	55	50	70	50	35	15	50	15	40	50	35	50	50	50	35	15	50	15	28	50
Dartmouth	The Dart Marina	44	25	59	25	44	25	59	25	37	25	44	25	59	25	44	25	59	25	37	25
Dorking	The White Horse	62	50	82	50	39	20	49	20	-	-	52	50	72	50	39	20	49	20	-	-
Dovedale	The Peveril of the Peak	42	10	57	10	42	10	57	10	35	10	39	10	54	10	39	10	54	10	32	10
Dunster	The Luttrell Arms	35	0	45	0	40	0	50	0	32	10	35	0	45	0	40	0	50	0	30	10
Exeter	The Southgate	60	30	70	30	50	20	55	20	40	30	60	30	70	30	40	20	50	20	45	30
Farnham	The Bush Hotel	87	50	107	50	39	20	49	20	-	-	77	50	97	50	39	20	49	20	-	-
Grasmere	The Swan	35	10	50	10	57	20	72	20	36	20	35	10	50	10	50	20	65	20	35	20
Helmsley	The Black Swan	45	20	65	20	60	20	80	20	48	20	40	20	60	20	52	20	72	20	40	20
Hereford	The Green Dragon	35	20	49	20	35	20	49	20	28	20	35	20	49	20	35	20	49	20	28	20
Hertingfordbury	The White Horse	65	40	80	40	42	0	54	0	48	40	65	40	80	40	40	0	50	0	47	40
Kingston	Kingston Lodge	70	50	85	50	40	20	55	20	-	-	70	50	85	50	40	20	55	20	-	-
Lavenham	The Swan	54	20	64	20	60	20	70	20	49	20	54	20	64	20	60	20	70	20	49	20
Lincoln	The White Hart	49	20	59	20	49	20	59	20	45	45	49	20	59	20	49	20	59	20	43	45
Marlborough	The Castle & Ball	30	20	45	20	30	15	45	15	23	20	30	20	45	20	30	15	45	15	23	20
Marlow	The Compleat Angler	75	60	90	60	70	25	90	25	65	60	75	60	85	60	70	25	90	25	65	60
Matlock	The New Bath Hotel	49	10	59	10	49	10	59	10	42	10	39	10	54	10	39	10	54	10	32	10
Mudeford	Avonmouth Hotel	40	20	54	20	45	20	59	20	30	20	35	20	49	20	40	20	54	20	30	20
North Berwick	The Marine	37	10	50	10	37	0	50	0	30	10	37	10	50	10	37	0	50	0	30	10
Oxford	Eastgate Hotel	50	25	65	25	50	25	65	25	43	30	55	25	70	25	55	25	70	25	48	30
Oxford	The Randolph	65	40	80	40	65	40	80	40	58	40	65	40	80	40	65	40	80	40	58	40
Padstow	The Metropole	35	20	45	20	40	20	49	20	35	20	35	20	45	20	40	20	49	20	33	20
Romsey	The White Horse	30	25	45	25	30	20	45	20	23	20	30	25	45	25	30	20	45	20	23	20
Ross on Wye	The Royal	45	10	57	10	45	10	57	10	38	10	45	10	57	10	45	10	57	10	38	10
St.Andrews	Rusacks Hotel	45	15	60	15	45	15	60	15	44	35	45	15	60	15	45	15	60	15	38	35
Salisbury	The White Hart	60	15	75	15	53	15	68	15	50	15	53	15	68	15	44	15	59	15	42	15
Sherborne	The Sherborne	30	15	40	15	30	15	40	15	23	15	30	15	40	15	30	15	40	15	23	15
Staines	The Thames Lodge	75	50	90	50	40	10	55	10	-	-	75	50	90	50	40	10	55	10	-	-
Stratford-upon-Avon	The Alveston Manor	65	20	80	20	69	20	80	20	60	20	65	20	80	20	65	20	80	20	58	20
Stratford-upon-Avon	The Shakespeare	79	30	94	30	79	30	94	30	72	30	79	30	94	30	79	30	94	30	72	30
Stratford-upon-Avon	The Swan's Nest	59	20	74	20	59	20	74	20	52	20	59	20	74	20	59	20	74	20	52	20
Ullswater	Leeming House	45	20	65	20	70	20	90	20	48	20	40	20	65	20	65	20	85	20	43	20
Winchester	The Wessex	54	50	69	50	49	20	64	20	45	20	54	50	69	50	49	20	59	20	43	20
Windermere	The Old England	39	20	54	20	54	20	69	20	37	20	39	20	54	20	49	20	64	20	37	20
Windsor	The Castle Hotel	75	50	89	50	55	20	70	20	-	-	85	50	99	50	49	20	65	20	-	-
Woodstock	The Bear	55	30	70	30	61	30	76	30	50	30	55	30	70	30	61	30	76	30	50	30
Worcester	The Giffard	35	0	47	0	35	0	47	0	28	10	35	0	47	0	35	0	47	0	28	10

KEY: BB – Bed & Breakfast   DBB – Dinner, Bed & Breakfast   PP – Per Person   SO – Sole Occupancy Supplement   † – Excluding 24-26 Dec   # – Excluding 30 Dec-2 Jan

For more information look on www.heritage-hotels.com or call 0345 404040

Location	Hotel	February 2000										March 2000									
		Midweek				Weekend				Weekaway		Midweek				Weekend				Weekaway	
		BB		DBB		BB		DBB		5 days or more BB		BB		DBB		BB		DBB		5 days or more BB	
		PP	SO	PP	SO	PP	SO	PP	SO	PP	SO	PP	SO	PP	SO	PP	SO	PP	SO	PP	SO
Abingdon	The Upper Reaches	56	20	71	20	56	25	71	25	49	20	67	20	82	20	67	25	82	25	60	20
Alfriston	The Star Inn	39	20	56	20	40	20	54	20	32	20	39	20	56	20	49	20	66	20	36	20
Amersham	The Crown	80	50	100	50	45	20	60	20	-	-	80	50	100	50	48	20	65	20	-	-
Ascot	The Berystede	85	50	99	20	49	20	65	20	-	-	85	50	99	20	55	20	70	20	-	-
Banbury	Whately Hall	50	40	65	40	40	15	55	10	40	40	50	40	65	40	40	15	55	10	40	40
Bath	The Francis	39	20	59	20	54	20	74	20	37	20	49	20	69	20	54	20	74	20	46	20
Bath	The Bath Spa	45	20	65	20	99	20	119	20	59	20	60	20	80	20	99	20	119	20	67	20
Box Hill	The Burford Bridge	85	50	99	50	49	20	59	20	-	-	85	50	99	50	49	20	59	20	-	-
Camberley	Frimley Hall	85	50	99	50	39	20	49	20	-	-	85	50	99	50	39	20	49	20	-	-
Canterbury	The Chaucer Hotel	45	30	55	30	45	30	55	30	37	30	49	30	59	30	49	30	59	30	42	30
Cheltenham	The Queen's	55	30	70	50	40	20	55	20	42	40	65	30	80	50	50	20	65	20	52	40
Chester	Blossoms Hotel	35	30	50	30	35	20	50	20	28	30	40	30	55	30	40	20	55	20	33	30
Coventry	Brandon Hall	55	50	70	50	35	15	50	15	40	50	55	50	70	50	35	15	50	15	40	50
Dartmouth	The Dart Marina	44	25	59	25	44	25	59	25	37	25	44	25	59	25	44	25	59	25	37	25
Dorking	The White Horse	52	50	72	50	39	20	49	20	-	-	62	50	82	50	39	20	49	20	-	-
Dovedale	The Peveril of the Peak	39	10	54	10	39	10	54	10	32	10	39	10	54	10	39	10	54	10	32	10
Dunster	The Luttrell Arms	35	0	45	0	40	0	50	0	30	10	35	0	50	0	45	0	55	0	33	10
Exeter	The Southgate	60	30	70	30	40	20	50	20	45	30	60	30	70	30	40	20	50	20	49	30
Farnham	The Bush Hotel	77	50	97	50	39	20	49	20	-	-	77	50	97	50	39	20	49	20	-	-
Grasmere	The Swan	40	10	55	10	50	20	65	20	38	20	45	10	60	10	63	20	78	20	45	20
Helmsley	The Black Swan	45	20	65	20	52	20	72	20	43	20	50	20	70	20	70	20	90	20	52	20
Hereford	The Green Dragon	35	20	49	20	35	20	49	20	28	20	42	20	58	20	42	20	58	20	35	20
Hertingfordbury	The White Horse	65	40	80	40	40	0	50	0	47	40	65	40	80	40	45	0	60	0	50	40
Kingston	Kingston Lodge	80	50	95	50	40	20	55	20	-	-	80	50	95	50	40	20	55	20	-	-
Lavenham	The Swan	54	20	64	20	60	20	70	20	49	20	56	20	66	20	60	20	70	20	50	20
Lincoln	The White Hart	49	20	59	20	49	20	59	20	43	45	59	20	65	20	59	20	65	20	53	45
Marlborough	The Castle & Ball	30	20	45	20	30	15	45	15	23	20	35	20	50	20	35	15	50	15	27	20
Marlow	The Compleat Angler	75	60	90	60	70	25	90	25	65	60	80	60	95	60	70	25	90	25	69	60
Matlock	The New Bath Hotel	39	10	54	10	39	10	54	10	32	10	39	10	54	10	39	10	54	10	32	10
Mudeford	Avonmouth Hotel	35	20	49	20	40	20	54	20	30	20	35	20	54	20	40	20	59	20	30	20
North Berwick	The Marine	42	10	57	10	42	0	57	0	35	10	42	10	57	10	42	0	57	0	35	10
Oxford	Eastgate Hotel	55	25	70	25	55	25	70	25	48	30	65	25	80	25	65	25	80	25	58	30
Oxford	The Randolph	65	40	80	40	65	40	80	40	58	40	78	40	93	40	65	40	80	40	65	40
Padstow	The Metropole	35	20	45	20	40	20	50	20	33	20	55	20	69	20	55	20	69	20	50	20
Romsey	The White Horse	30	25	45	25	30	20	45	20	23	20	35	25	50	25	35	20	50	20	27	20
Ross on Wye	The Royal	45	10	57	10	45	10	57	10	38	10	47	10	59	10	49	10	59	10	40	10
St.Andrews	Rusacks Hotel	45	15	60	15	45	15	60	15	38	35	50	15	65	15	50	15	65	15	42	35
Salisbury	The White Hart	53	15	68	15	44	15	59	15	42	15	53	15	68	15	53	15	68	15	47	15
Sherborne	The Sherborne	30	15	40	15	30	15	40	15	23	15	40	15	50	15	40	15	50	15	33	15
Staines	The Thames Lodge	75	50	90	50	40	10	55	10	-	-	80	50	95	50	40	10	55	10	-	-
Stratford-upon-Avon	The Alveston Manor	65	20	80	20	65	20	80	20	58	20	79	20	99	20	74	20	89	20	70	20
Stratford-upon-Avon	The Shakespeare	79	30	94	30	79	30	94	30	72	30	84	30	105	30	84	30	99	30	77	30
Stratford-upon-Avon	The Swan's Nest	59	20	74	20	59	20	74	20	52	20	69	20	84	20	N/A	20	79	20	62	20
Ullswater	Leeming House	40	20	60	20	65	20	85	20	43	20	55	20	75	20	70	20	90	20	55	20
Winchester	The Wessex	54	50	69	50	44	20	59	20	43	20	64	50	79	50	54	20	69	20	53	20
Windermere	The Old England	39	20	54	20	49	20	64	20	37	20	45	20	60	20	63	20	78	20	45	20
Windsor	The Castle Hotel	85	50	99	50	49	20	65	20	-	-	85	50	99	50	55	20	70	20	-	-
Woodstock	The Bear	55	30	70	30	61	30	76	30	50	30	65	30	80	30	70	30	87	30	60	30
Worcester	The Giffard	35	0	47	0	35	0	47	0	28	10	35	0	47	0	35	0	47	0	28	10

KEY: BB – Bed & Breakfast   DBB – Dinner, Bed & Breakfast   PP – Per Person   SO – Sole Occupancy Supplement

For more information look on www.heritage-hotels.com or call 0345 404040

137

Terms & Conditions

The Terms & Conditions detailed below apply to all Short Breaks and Holidays featured in this brochure excluding Christmas and Millennium breaks. For a copy of our Christmas and Millennium Celebrations brochure, please call 0345 700 350 quoting MH1. When you make a booking, your contract will be with Forte (UK) Ltd ('Forte'), 166 High Holborn, London, WC1V 6TT, England.

1. AVAILABILITY

All Short Breaks and Holidays featured in this brochure are offered subject to availability. Bookings can be made for stays commencing from May 1st 1999 to February 29th 2000 inclusive, excluding December 24th–26th and December 30th – January 2nd.

2. HOLIDAY TYPES AND LENGTH OF STAY

The main holiday types are:

- Midweek Leisure Break – one or more consecutive nights between Monday and Thursday inclusive.
- Weekend Leisure Break – one or more consecutive nights between Friday and Sunday inclusive. (Weekend Leisure Breaks also include Bank Holiday Mondays).
- Half Price Sunday Nights – if you book a weekend leisure break on either a bed & breakfast or dinner, bed & breakfast basis for a Friday and Saturday night - you can stay on Sunday night at 50% of the weekend leisure break price.
- Weekaways – great value Bed & Breakfast package for 5 nights or more – a reduction on normal Bed & Breakfast prices.

One night stays are available on all products available in this brochure (excluding Half Price Sunday Nights and Weekaways).

3. PRICING

All prices shown in this brochure are in £'s per person per night (unless otherwise indicated) sharing a twin/double room or for one person in a single room. If staying as a single guest, a single occupancy supplement may apply (please see Single Guests below). For further information, please see the hotel listing information pricing panels, or call **Forte Central Reservations on 0345 40 40 40.**

All **Short Breaks and Holidays** prices in this brochure include all taxes and non-optional service charges. Forte reserves the right to increase or decrease brochure prices to reflect any change in tax rates which occur after May 1st 1999. Once your contract is concluded, there will be no price changes.

4. WHAT'S INCLUDED IN THE PRICE

All Short Breaks & Holidays include comfortable, well-appointed accommodation sharing a twin/double room (single room for single guests) with colour TV, tea and coffee making facilities*, direct dial telephone, private en suite bathroom and continental or full traditional breakfast each morning. Guests staying on dinner, bed and breakfast breaks additionally receive a three course dinner with tea or coffee each day.

5. *TEA & COFFEE MAKING FACILITIES

Tea & coffee making facilities are available at all Heritage hotels. At The Randolph Hotel in Oxford and The Bath Spa Hotel in Bath – tea & coffee making facilities should be requested on arrival.

6. FEATURE ROOMS

At many Heritage Hotels, you can upgrade your accommodation to a feature room from £7.50 per person per night. Feature rooms may have a spectacular view, extra facilities or a four poster or half tester bed.

7. SINGLE GUESTS

Individual guests using a single room are charged the standard per person rate as shown in the price panel. When no single room is available individual guests may book a double or twin room and pay the sole occupancy supplement as shown for the relevant hotel.

8. CHILDREN

At all Heritage Hotels, up to 2 children under 16 stay free when sharing a suitable room with up to 2 adults (or one adult if a single parent family), subject to availability. Children who occupy their own room will be charged 75% of the appropriate adult inclusive price. Cots and high chairs are available free of charge at all hotels.

9. BABY LISTENING & BABYSITTING

Baby listening is available free of charge at most hotels when advance notice is given. At some hotels, baby-sitting is also available as a chargeable extra. Where available, 14 days advance notice is required by calling the hotel direct. For more information on any individual hotel, please call Forte Central Reservations on 0345 40 40 40.

10. GUESTS WITH IMPAIRED MOBILITY

A number of Heritage hotels offer modified facilities for guests with impaired mobility. Others, whilst not having special facilities, have mainly level access to public areas and accessible bathrooms. Please call Forte Central Reservations on 0345 40 40 40 for further information of the facilities at the hotel where you intend to stay.

11. GUIDE DOGS

All Heritage Hotels accept guide dogs at no extra charge. Guide dogs are allowed in the public areas. Owners are responsible for making good the cost of any damage.

12. DOGS

Certain Heritage Hotels, at the manager's discretion, can accommodate dogs in some cases for an extra charge. Please call Forte Central Reservations on 0345 40 40 40 to enquire about the hotel where you intend to stay. Dogs are not allowed in the public areas and owners are responsible for making good the cost of any damage.

13. CAR PARKING

Car parking is free at most Heritage hotels, but at some sites there is limited availability. For further information on parking availability and charges, please call direct to the hotel of your intended stay on its enquiries number.

14. CHECKING IN & CHECKING OUT

Arrival: Hotel rooms are available from 14:00 on the day of arrival. Guests are asked to inform the hotel if arrival after 18:00 is anticipated.

Departure: Rooms must be vacated by 12:00 on the day of departure unless otherwise sanctioned at the discretion of the Hotel Manager.

15. MEAL ARRANGEMENTS

All Short Breaks and Holidays which include breakfast offer a full traditional or continental breakfast with tea or coffee.

All Short Breaks and Holidays which include dinner offer a choice from the hotel's three course evening menu. If a hotel does not provide a three course menu, guests may select a recognised starter, main course and dessert. A la carte dining is available at some hotels for an extra charge. All dinners include tea or coffee. Additional beverages are chargeable extras.

There is no refund for meals not taken and lunch cannot be taken in place of dinner.

16. TOURING HOLIDAYS

'Touring Holidays' are for a minimum of 5 consecutive nights and itineraries are tailor made to your individual requirements. Once you have planned your route and chosen your hotels from the brochure, please call Forte Inclusive Packages on 0345 543 555 who will calculate the price of your holiday.

17. HERITAGE HOTELS 'BREAK FOR MURDER'

All 'Break for Murder' weekends include a welcome reception, two nights dinner, bed and breakfast accommodation sharing a twin or double room with colour TV, tea and coffee making facilities*, telephone, private en suite bathroom, and lunch on Saturday. Weekends also include a 'Break for Murder' programme with competitions, games and 'murders' appropriate to each plot, with actors to provide the entertainment and guide you through the murder plot.

'Break for Murder' operates according to a minimum and maximum group size to ensure that all participants benefit fully from the programme. If the appropriate numbers are not achieved, Forte reserve the right to cancel the break by giving at least two weeks' advance notice (usually longer) and, where possible, offering an alternative date or venue. Should these alternatives not be suitable, all moneys paid will be refunded. 'Break for Murder' is not suitable for children under 16.

18. HERITAGE HOTELS 'MUSIC AT LEISURE'

Music at Leisure weekends include programmes, a champagne reception on Friday and Saturday evenings, 2 nights accommodation sharing a twin or double room with private bathroom (or a single room), full traditional breakfast each morning, three course evening meal with coffee. The weekends operate according to minimum party size. If the appropriate numbers are not achieved, Forte reserve the right to cancel the break by giving at least two weeks' advance notice (usually longer) and, where possible, offering an alternative date or venue. Should these alternatives not be suitable, all moneys paid will be refunded.

19. HEALTH AND FITNESS CLUBS

A charge may be made for the use of certain facilities eg solaria, exercise classes and beauty treatments.

Under 16's are not permitted to use the gymnasium and must be accompanied by a responsible adult at all times when using the other facilities.

Under 5's are not permitted to use spa pools, saunas, solaria and steam rooms.

20. GENERAL INFORMATION

Brochure details apply to reservations made on or before February 29th 2000 subject to publication of subsequent editions of this supplement.

All information is correct as at May 1st 1999 but is subject to change before your contract is concluded.

The photographs, illustrations and descriptions of facilities, amenities, surrounding areas and places of interest are reproduced in this brochure to give a general impression of what to expect on your chosen short break or holiday and should not be taken as a guarantee of what will be available.

Forte cannot be held responsible for events beyond its control or the control of its suppliers (such as fire, strikes, industrial action, terrorist activity, technical problems with transport, Illness of entertainers and/or sporting supervisors and bad weather), nor for any curtailment, cancellation or change to any accommodation, activity or itinerary which is caused as a result of such events.

21. YEAR 2000 DATE RECOGNITION

Forte has taken all reasonable care to try to ensure that its computer systems and other relevant technologies are Millennium compliant. Forte is also asking all their suppliers to try to ensure that their own systems have been checked and adapted where necessary to cope with the potential problems which the Year 2000 date change may cause. However, this is a complex problem and Forte cannot accept liability if problems occur as a result of any date recognition failure, although Forte will try to minimise any difficulties resulting from them should they occur.

22. COMPLAINTS & COMMENTS

Any complaint or comment regarding a stay at a hotel should be made to the hotel's Duty Manager at the time of the visit so that it can be resolved on the spot. Problems which cannot be resolved there and then should be notified in writing, within 28 days of departure, to the following: Managing Director, Heritage Hotels, 166, High Holborn, London, WC1V 6TT.

BOOKING INFORMATION

1. HOW TO BOOK

There are four ways to make a booking:-
- Call Forte Central Reservations on 0345 40 40 40; or
- Call the hotel of your intended stay; or
- Contact your travel agent; or
- For Touring Holidays, Murder Breaks and Music at Leisure packages call Forte Inclusive Packages on 0345 543 555

If you make a booking through Forte Central Reservations or direct with the hotel, you will be asked to guarantee your booking with a credit/debit card. If you do not possess a credit/debit card, you will be required to pre-pay by cheque (made payable to Forte (UK) Ltd). To pre-pay by cheque, please complete and sign the booking form on the back cover of this supplement and send it along with your cheque to the hotel of your intended stay. You will find the address printed in the hotel listing information. Where pre-payment by cheque is necessary,

at least three working days following receipt of your cheque will be required to process the transaction prior to your stay commencing.

If you make a 'Touring Holiday' booking through Forte Inclusive Packages on 0345 543 555 you will be required to pre-pay in full for your break. For 'Murder Breaks' and 'Music at Leisure' weekends, a deposit of 20% is required. Please complete and sign the booking form on the back cover of this supplement, and send it along with your credit/debit card details, or cheque made payable to Forte (UK) Ltd, to Forte Inclusive Packages, Oak Court, Dudley Road, Brierly Hill, West Midlands, DY5 1LG. Where pre-payment is by cheque, at least three working days will be required following receipt of your cheque to process the transaction prior to your stay commencing.

If you make a booking through a travel agent, please complete and sign the booking form on the back cover of this brochure including your payment details and give this to your travel agent. Your travel agent will do the rest.

2. IMPORTANT INFORMATION REGARDING AVAILABILITY

Heavy demand at certain times of the year may mean that some rooms may not be available at the special prices featured in this brochure. In the case of facilities/services not provided by Forte, prices are subject to change before the contract is concluded. Forte will inform guests of these changes. Your travel agent will be pleased to confirm and offer alternative dates and hotels if necessary. Receipt of payment does not guarantee availability.

3. DEPOSITS AND PRE-PAYMENT

Deposits and pre-payments are not required for most of the Short Breaks and Holidays featured in this brochure. Deposits and pre-payments are, however, required when making bookings for all 'Touring Holidays', 'Break for Murder' and 'Music at Leisure' weekends.

When booking a 'Touring Holiday', the full price of the holiday and the special delivery post supplement must be pre-paid in full prior to your stay commencing. Payment can be made by credit/debit card or by cheque (made payable to Forte (UK) Ltd) to: Forte Inclusive Packages, Oak Court, Dudley Road, Brierley Hill, West Midlands, DY5 1LG.

When booking a Heritage Hotels 'Break for Murder' or 'Music at Leisure' weekend, a deposit of 20% of the holiday price is required. Payment, by credit/debit card or cheque (made payable to Forte (UK) Ltd), should be sent to the hotel direct and the address will be advised at the time of making the booking.

When making a booking through a travel agent, the agent will take deposits and final balance payments according to the travel agent's normal practice. All bookings must be pre-paid in full prior to commencing your stay.

4. BALANCE OF MONEYS OUTSTANDING

Prior to your departure from the hotel you will be required to settle your bill. If your reservation was made through a travel agent, you will be required to pay for all extra services consumed during your stay that were

not included in your pre-paid Short Break or Holiday. If your reservation was made direct with Forte you will be required to pay for the Short Break or Holiday in full, less any pre-payments, plus any extra services consumed during your stay.

On arrival, you will be asked to produce a valid credit card for the hotel to take an imprint. Forte accepts all major credit cards including MasterCard, Visa, American Express and Diners Club. Alternatively, payment may be made by cheque, payable to Forte (UK) Ltd. All cheques must be supported by, and within the limits of, a current cheque card and above this limit, they are accepted only by prior arrangement with the hotel. Where pre-payment by cheque is necessary, at least three working days will be required to process the transaction.

5. CANCELLATION & AMENDMENTS

There is no charge if you wish to cancel your booking up to 14:00 on the day of arrival. In the event of cancellation after 14:00 or non-arrival, Forte reserves the right to charge you for one night's accommodation.

'TOURING HOLIDAYS', 'MUSIC AT LEISURE' AND 'BREAK FOR MURDER'
In the event of a guest cancelling any of the above mentioned holidays, 20% of the total holiday price will be retained as a cancellation charge. A cancellation reference will be given and should be retained.

TICKETS
Once issued, all tickets for theatre performances, concerts and events booked through Forte cannot be amended and no refunds will be made.

REFUND OF MONEYS PAID
The balance of moneys paid, less any cancellation charges and the cost of any tickets, will be refunded on receipt of all documentation and tickets either by your travel agent or at Forte (UK) Ltd, Oak Court, Dudley Road, Brierley Hill, West Midlands, DY5 1LG.

6. HOLIDAY & TRAVEL INSURANCE

Forte (UK) Ltd strongly recommend that all guests take out adequate holiday/travel insurance when booking any of the short breaks and holidays featured in this brochure. Forte (UK) Ltd have arranged a special facility with Aon Cork Bays & Fisher of Lloyds Chambers, 1 Portsoken Street, London, E1 8DF, England. Please call 0171 680 4000 or ask your travel agent for further information and prices.

7. BOOKING AFTERTHOUGHTS

Should you have any post-booking queries, please call Forte Central Reservations on 0345 40 40 40 or the hotel direct quoting your booking reference number. If your booking was made through a travel agent, please contact your travel agent quoting your booking reference number.

8. SECURITY FOR MONEYS PAID OVER

Under government regulations, Forte (UK) Ltd is required to provide insurance, in relation to certain packages, for security of money paid over by guests and for their repatriation in the unlikely event of insolvency of the company. This insurance is arranged by:
Aon Risk Services Ltd of Lloyds Chambers, 1 Portsoken Street, London, E1 8DF. Telephone 0171 680 4000.

We offer a relaxing alternative to the exhausting ritual of Christmas at home, plus an exciting once-in-your-lifetime celebration of the millennium.

A TRADITIONAL CHRISTMAS

Three-nights accommodation for 24 through 26 December with all the trimmings — a warm reception on Christmas Eve, a visit from Santa, carol ringers, carol singers and every meal right up through the Boxing Day Buffet

PEACE & QUIET CHRISTMAS

A relaxed, toned-down holiday celebration 24–26 December in a lovely ambiance. All meals, including morning coffee, afternoon tea and Boxing Day lunch and dinner.

MILLENNIUM CELEBRATION

Welcome 2000 in Heritage House style at one of our charming hotels. Our package includes a champagne reception, New Year's Eve dinner, a midnight celebration, fireworks (at selected hotels), and a full traditional breakfast on New Year's Day.

MILLENNIUM HOUSE PARTY

Take over one of eleven Heritage Hotels with your friends and family. We will help you create an imaginative and memorable celebration. Packages will vary by hotel, but include three-nights accommodation, all meals and entertainment.

To discuss our holiday packages and the specific hotels and locations in which they are offered, call 034 540 4040.

Key to Maps

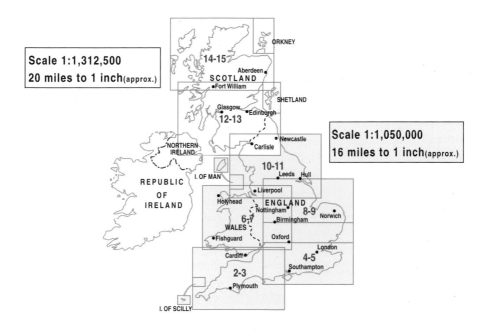

Scale 1:1,312,500
20 miles to 1 inch(approx.)

ORKNEY

14-15

Aberdeen
SCOTLAND
•Fort William

SHETLAND

Glasgow
•Edinburgh
12-13

Scale 1:1,050,000
16 miles to 1 inch(approx.)

NORTHERN
IRELAND

Newcastle
•Carlisle

10-11
Leeds Hull

•Liverpool

REPUBLIC
OF
IRELAND

I. OF MAN

Holyhead

ENGLAND
Nottingham
•Birmingham

8-9
Norwich

6-7
WALES
•Fishguard

Oxford

London

Cardiff•
2-3
•Plymouth

4-5
Southampton

I. OF SCILLY

Legend

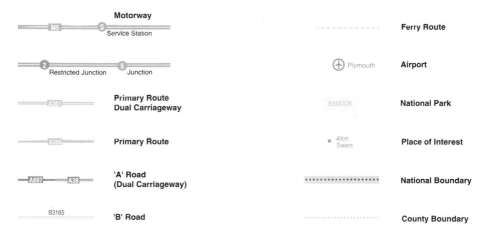

Motorway / Service Station	**Ferry Route**
Restricted Junction / Junction	Plymouth **Airport**
Primary Route Dual Carriageway	EXMOOR **National Park**
Primary Route	Alton Towers **Place of Interest**
A697 — A38 **'A' Road (Dual Carriageway)**	**National Boundary**
B3165 **'B' Road**	**County Boundary**

© West One 1999

Page	Hotel name	Page	Hotel name
28	The Bath Spa Hotel	76	The Castle & Ball
30	The Francis	84	The Avonmouth Hotel
46	The Dart Marina	92	The Metropolo
54	The Luttrell Arms	102	The White Hart
56	The Southgate	104	The Sherborne

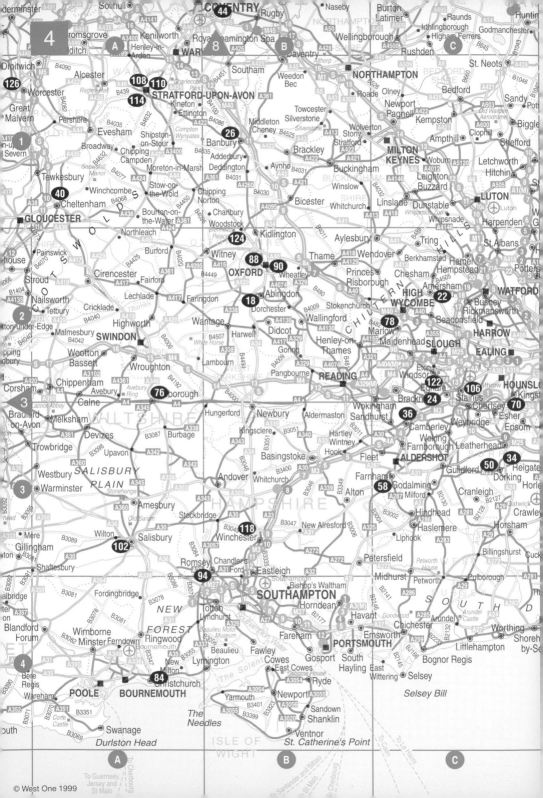

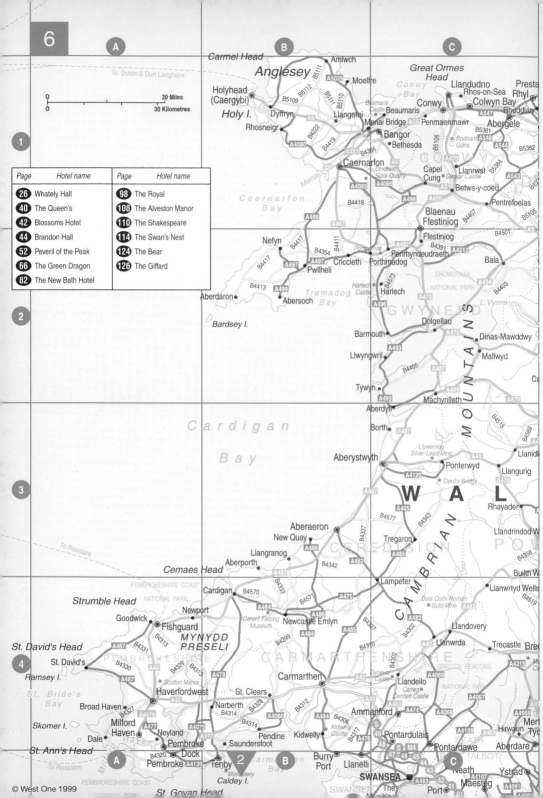

6

20 Miles
30 Kilometres

© West One 1999

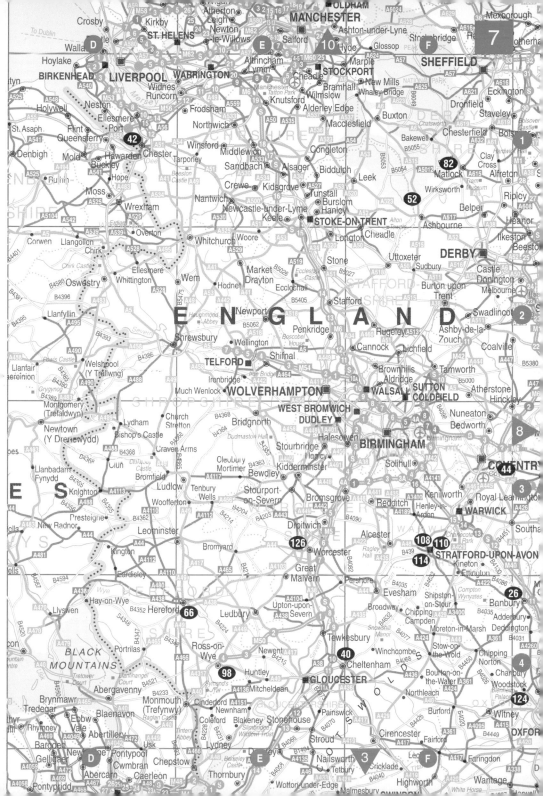

8

Burnley Hebden BRADFORD Morley Rothwell Castleford Howden South Cave UPON HULL Hedon
Halifax Brighouse Knottingley Goole Barton-upon-Humberside New Holland Patringto
Elland Dewsbury Wakefield Pontefract 11 Winterton Scunthorpe Immingha
HUDDERSFIELD Holmfirth Adwick le Street Hatfield Thorne Crowle Brigg Caistor
BARNSLEY Bentley Doncaster Belton Kirton in Lindsey
MANCHESTER Ashton-under-Lyne Mexborough Conisbrough Market Rasen
Hyde Glossop Stocksbridge Rawmarsh Rotherham Tickhill Bawtry Gainsborough Woodhall Spa
Marple New Mills SHEFFIELD Maltby Wragby Horncastle
STOCKPORT Dronfield Dinnington Worksop East Retford Lincoln 74
Bramhall Eckington Staveley A632 Ollerton Boughton Swinderby Sleaford
Wilmslow Chesterfield Bolsover Mansfield Woodhouse Newark-on-Trent Cranwell
Alderley Edge Bakewell Clay Cross MANSFIELD Southwell Donington
Macclesfield Buxton 82 Matlock Alfreton Sutton in Ashfield Grantham
Congleton Wirksworth 52 Belper Ripley Kirkby in Ashfield Hucknall Arnold Bingham
Leek Ashbourne Heanor Carlton
STOKE-ON-TRENT Cheadle Ilkeston Beeston NOTTINGHAM Grantham
Longton DERBY Long Eaton West Bridgford Croxton Kerrial
Stone Uttoxeter Sudbury Castle Donington Melbourne East Midlands Corby Glen
GLAND Stafford Burton upon Trent Swadlincote Shepshed Loughborough Melton Mowbray Bourne Market Deeping
Rugeley Ashby-de-la-Zouch Coalville Mountsorrel Cottesmore Stamford
Cannock Lichfield Syston Thurmaston Oakham Duddington PETER
Brownhills Tamworth LEICESTER Uppingham Wansford
Aldridge Atherstone Oadby Stilton
WALSALL SUTTON COLDFIELD Hinckley Wigston Corby Oundle Ramsey
EST BROMWICH Nuneaton Market Harborough Desborough Thrapston Huntin
DUDLEY Bedworth Lutterworth Kettering Rauns Godmanchester
Halesowen BIRMINGHAM Husband's Bosworth Rothwell Naseby Burton Latimer Irthlingborough Higham Ferrers
Hagley Solihull COVENTRY 44 Rugby Wellingborough Rushden St. Neots
Bromsgrove Redditch Kenilworth Royal Leamington Spa Daventry NORTHAMPTON Bedford Sandy
Worcester 108 110 Henley-in-Arden WARWICK Southam Weedon Bec Olney Newport Pagnell Kempston Shefford
26 Alcester 114 STRATFORD-UPON-AVON Kineton Ettington Towcester Wolverton Ampthill Biggle
Pershore Evesham Shipston-on-Stour Banbury 26 Middleton Cheney Silverstone Stony Stratford MILTON KEYNES Letchworth Hitchin
Broadway Chipping Campden Moreton-in-Marsh Adderbury Brackley Buckingham Woburn LUTON
Tewkesbury Winchcombe Stow-on-the-Wold Deddington Aynho Winslow Leighton Buzzard Linslade Dunstable Harpenden
40 Cheltenham Bourton-on-the-Water Chipping Norton Bicester Whitchurch Whipsnade
GLOUCESTER Northleach Charlbury Woodstock Kidlington

9

© West One 1999

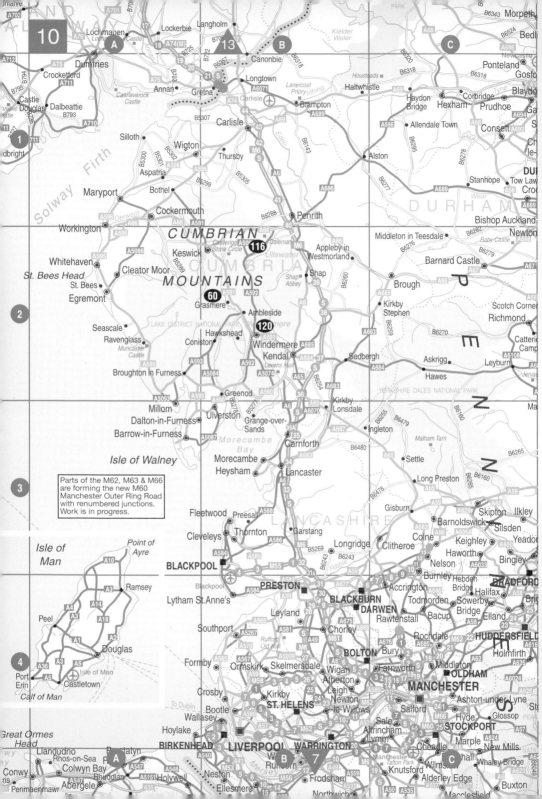

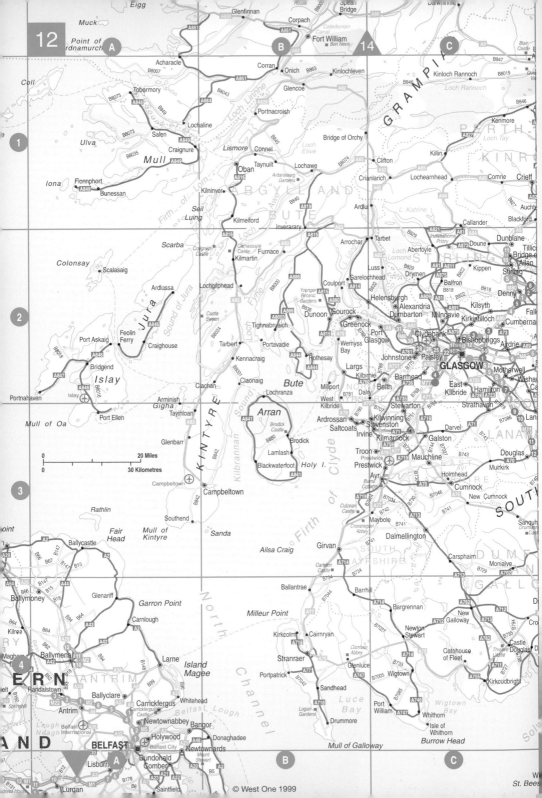

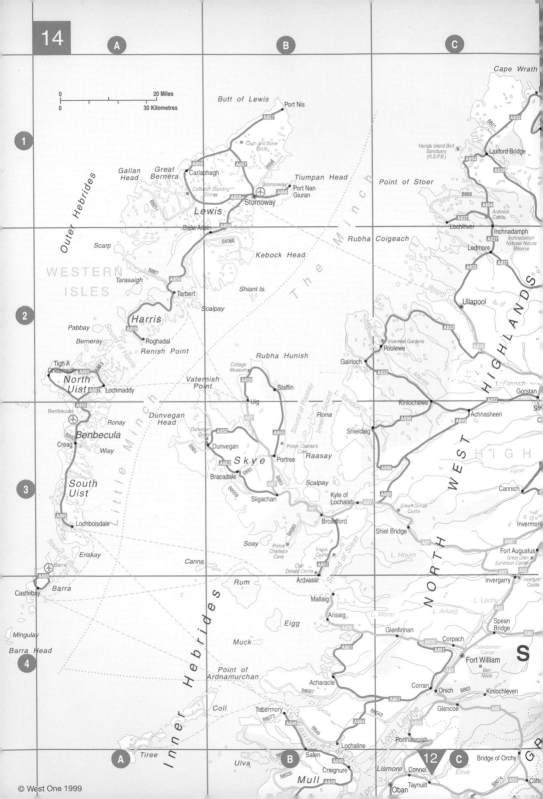

© West One 1999

A B C

1

2

3

4

Cape Wrath

Handa Island Bird
Sanctuary
(R.S.P.B.)

Laxford Bridge
B801
A838

B869

A894

Ardvreck
Castle

Lochinver

Inchnadamph
Inchnadamph
National Nature
Reserve

A837

Ledmore
A835

A837

Ullapool
A832

A835

Point of Stoer

Butt of Lewis
A857
Port Nis
**Port Nan
Giuran**

Tiumpan Head

Cairn and Stone
Circle
A857
B895

Carlabhagh
A858

Callanish Standing
Stones
B871

**Great
Bernera**

**Gallan
Head**

Stornoway
A866
A859

Lewis

Baile Ailein
A859

B8060

Kebock Head

Rubha Coigeach

The Minch

Outer Hebrides

Scarp

**WESTERN
ISLES**

Tarasaigh
B887

Harris
A859

Tarbert
A859

Scalpay

Shiant Is.

Rubha Hunish

Cottage
Museum

Staffin
A855

Uig
A87

Roghadal
A859

Renish Point

Pabbay

Berneray

Sound of Harris

**Vaternish
Point**

**Dunvegan
Head**

Dunvegan
Castle
A850

Dunvegan
B884

Skye
A863

Bracadale
B885

B8009

Sligachan
A863

Soay

Prince
Charles's
Cave

Rona

Portree
A855

Prince Charles's Cave

Raasay

Sound of Raasay

Scalpay
A87

**Kyle of
Lochalsh**
A87

Broadford
A851
B8083

Knock
Castle

Clan
Donald Centre

Ardvasar
A851

**Tigh A
Ghearraidh**
A865
Lochmaddy
A867

North Uist
A865

Ronay

Benbecula

Creag
B892

Wiay

Benbecula

**South
Uist**
A865

Lochboisdale
A865

Eriskay

Little Minch

Sound of Barra

Barra

Castlebay
A888

Barra

Mingulay

Barra Head

Inner Hebrides

Canna

Rum

Eigg

Muck

**Point of
Ardnamurchan**

Coll

Tobermory
B8073
A848

Ulva

Mull
A849

Salen
B849

Craignure
B8035
A849

Mallaig

Arisaig
A830

Glenfinnan
A830
A861

Acharacle
B8007
A861

Lochaline
B8043
B849

Corran
A861

Onich
B863

Glencoe
A82

L. Morar

L. Arkaig

Lismore

Connel

Taynuilt

Oban

Kinlochewe
A832
A896

Achnasheen
A890
A832

Shieldaig
A896

Gorstan
A835

Str

Cannich

Invermor

Shiel Bridge
A87

Fort Augustus
A82
A887
Great Glen
Exhibition Centre

Invergarry
A82
Invergar
Castle

**Spean
Bridge**
A86

Corpach
A830
Caledonian
Canal
A861

Fort William
A82
Ben
Nevis

Kinlochleven

Bridge of Orchy

Gairloch
A832

Poolewe
Inverewe Gardens

Eilean Donan
Castle

**NORTH
WEST
HIGHLANDS**

HIGH

L. Broom

L. Maree

L. Torridon

Inner Sound

Loch Linnhe

L. Hourn

L. Lochy

L. Etive

The Minch

20 Miles
30 Kilometres

12

S

G

Farrat

Portnacroish
B828

Taynuilt

Clifh
B8074

Bridge of Orchy

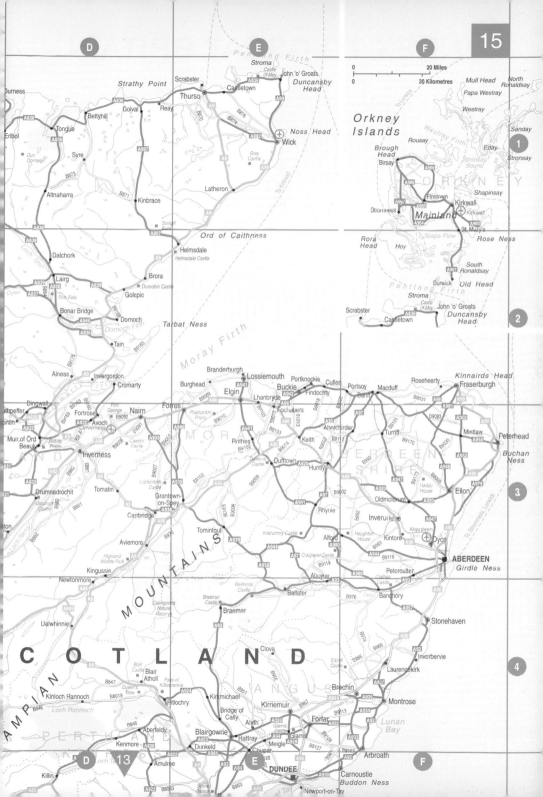

INDEX TO GREAT BRITAIN

Abbreviations of County and new Unitary Authority names used in this index.

Aber	= Aberdeenshire	Guer	= Guernsey	Oxon	= Oxfordshire
Arg	= Argyll & Bute	Hants	= Hampshire	Pemb	= Pembrokeshire
Brid	= Bridgend	Herts	= Hertfordshire	S Lan	= South Lanarkshire
Bucks	= Buckinghamshire	High	= Highland	S York	= South Yorkshire
Camb	= Cambridgeshire	IoM	= Isle of Man	Shrop	= Shropshire
Corn	= Cornwall	IoW	= Isle of Wight	Som	= Somerset
Derb	= Derbyshire	Jer	= Jersey	Staf	= Staffordshire
Dor	= Dorset	Linc	= Lincolnshire	Suff	= Suffolk
Dur	= Durham	Med	= Medway Towns	W Isl	= Western Isles
E York	= East Riding of Yorkshire	New	= Newport	W York	= West Yorkshire
G Man	= Greater Manchester	Norf	= Norfolk	Wrek	= The Wrekin
Glos	= Gloucestershire	North	= Northamptonshire		

Picture Credits

p 9 t, m, b: ©Spectrum Colour Library

pp 4, 23 t, 25 t, 35 b, 37 b, 41 b, 67 b, 73 b, 89 t, 93 b, 99 t, 99 b, 101 b 103 t, 121 t, 127 t: ©The Travel Library/Greg Evans Int

pp 19 t, 21 t, 29 b, 31 t, 37 t, 39 t, 55 t, 55 b, 61 b, 63 b, 77 b, 85 t, 85 b, 91, 83 t, 93 t, 125 t: ©The Travel Library

pp 19 b, 29 t, 45 t, 45 b, 51 b, 53 t, 47 b, 57 t, 71 b, 75 b, 83 b, 91 t, 103 b, 109 t, 121 b, 127 b: ©The Travel Library/Roger Howard

p 21 b: ©The Travel Library/A. Amsel

pp 23 b, 27 t, 39 b, 41 t, 43 b, 47 t, 53 b, 63 t, 67 t, 69 t, 69 b, 75 t, 79 b, 87 b, 95 t, 101 t, 105 t, 107 t, 111 b, 117 b, 109 b, 111 t, 115 b, 123 l: ©The Travel Library/R. Richardson

pp 25 b, 35 t: ©The Travel Library/Neil Egerton

p 27 b: ©The Travel Library/John Colley

pp 31 t, 59 b, 79 t, 105 b, 107b, 119 t, 123 r: ©The Travel Library/Philip Enticknap

p 43 t: ©The Travel Library/David Toase

pp 51 t, 89 b, 115 t: ©The Travel Library/David McGill

p 57 b: ©The Travel Library/John Welbum

p 59 t: ©The Travel Library/Peter Terry

pp 61 t, 77 t, 73 t, 119 b: ©The Travel Library/Stuart Black

pp 71 t, 125 b: ©The Travel Library/Mike Kipling

p 87 t: ©The Travel Library/Pete Trafford

p95 b: ©The Travel Library/G. Walden

p 117 t: ©The Travel Library/L. Garland